How to Love with AuDHD

A Practical Guide to Authentic Relationships for Those with Autism and ADHD

Gaetana Yo Tate

Copyright © 2024 by Gaetana Yo Tate

All rights reserved. No part of this publication may be reproduced, distributed, or transmitted in any form or by any means without the prior written permission of the authors, except in the case of brief quotations in critical reviews.

This book is for educational purposes only and is not intended as medical, psychological, or professional advice. The authors are not licensed medical or mental health professionals. Consult qualified healthcare providers before making decisions about mental health, relationships, or medical care.

Strategies described may not work for everyone. Individual results vary, and the authors make no guarantees about effectiveness.

All names, case studies, and examples (including Sarah, Marcus, Jordan, Alex, River, Cam, Quinn, Reese, Avery, Taylor, Morgan, Casey, Sam, Riley, Phoenix, Sage, Dakota, Cameron, Emma, David, Michael, Tom, Lisa, Jennifer, Jake, Maria, Anna, Mark, Rachel, and all other named individuals) are fictional composites created for illustration. Any resemblance to actual persons is purely coincidental.

Terms like "autism," "ADHD," "AuDHD," and "neurodivergent" are used according to community understanding and are not diagnostic tools. Proper diagnosis requires professional evaluation.

The authors and publisher disclaim liability for any adverse effects arising from use of this information, including relationship difficulties, emotional distress, or other negative outcomes.

ISBN: 978-1-7642235-7-7
Isohan Publishing

Table of Contents

Chapter 1: When autism meets ADHD in your heart 1

Chapter 2: The vulnerability factor no one talks about 11

Chapter 3: Rejection sensitivity and the fear of being "too much" ... 23

Chapter 4: Unmasking your way to real intimacy 36

Chapter 5: Communication when words are hard 50

Chapter 6: Sensory intimacy and physical connection 61

Chapter 7: Executive function hacks for two 74

Chapter 8: Creating your relationship user manual 87

Chapter 9: The conflict resolution remix 99

Chapter 10: Managing energy as a finite resource 112

Chapter 11: Building routines that flex 125

Chapter 12: Social life and couple boundaries 138

Chapter 13: When both partners are neurodivergent 151

Chapter 14: Trauma, healing, and moving forward 165

Chapter 15: Growing through life transitions 179

Chapter 16: Creating a sensory sanctuary together 193

Chapter 17: Long-term love with AuDHD 203

Chapter 18: Your authentic love story 214

Reference 226

Chapter 1: When autism meets ADHD in your heart

Love gets complicated when your brain runs on two different operating systems at once. You might find yourself desperately craving routine while simultaneously feeling bored by predictability. Or maybe you love your partner deeply but feel overwhelmed by their presence. This isn't contradiction—this is AuDHD in relationships.

Most people think having both autism and ADHD means you get a little of each condition. The reality hits different. AuDHD creates an entirely new experience that goes beyond simple addition. Your relationship challenges don't just multiply—they transform into something altogether unique.

AuDHD is not just autism + ADHD: The multiplier effect on relationships

Traditional relationship advice assumes everyone processes connection the same way. You know better. Your brain processes love through both autism's need for depth and ADHD's hunger for stimulation. This creates relationship experiences that neurotypical couples never encounter.

Research shows that 50-70% of autistic individuals also have ADHD traits. But these aren't separate conditions running parallel tracks in your mind. They interact, conflict, and sometimes amplify each other in ways that change everything about how you love and connect.

Consider Sarah, a 28-year-old marketing professional who describes her relationship experience: "I need my boyfriend to be completely predictable so I feel safe, but I also need him to surprise me or I get bored. I want deep conversations about feelings, but I can't sit still long enough to have them. I love being close to him, but his breathing sounds make me want to crawl out of my skin."

Sarah's experience demonstrates the multiplier effect. Her autism craves emotional safety through routine and predictability. Her ADHD demands novelty and stimulation. Her sensory processing differences affect physical intimacy. These aren't three separate issues—they're one complex system that requires entirely different approaches than typical relationship advice offers.

The multiplier effect shows up in communication too. You might have autism's tendency toward literal interpretation combined with ADHD's impulsive responses. This means you both miss subtle social cues AND react quickly to what you think you heard. The result? Misunderstandings that escalate faster than either partner can process.

The push-pull paradox: Craving routine AND novelty simultaneously

Your internal world contains what feels like two different people with opposite needs. One part of you thrives on routine, predictability, and detailed planning. The other part feels trapped by schedules and craves spontaneous adventures. This isn't personality quirks—this is neurological reality.

Marcus, a 34-year-old teacher, explains: "Every Friday, my wife and I order pizza and watch a movie. I love this routine—it makes me feel secure and connected. But by the third Friday in a row, I'm dying to do something different. I want to keep the tradition AND break it simultaneously. My wife thinks I'm being difficult, but I literally need both things."

The push-pull paradox affects relationship planning in specific ways:

- **Date planning becomes impossible** because you want both structure and spontaneity
- **Vacation planning triggers internal conflict** between detailed itineraries and flexible exploration
- **Social events feel overwhelming** when you need both preparation time and room for changes
- **Daily routines provide comfort** while also feeling restrictive

Understanding this paradox helps both you and your partner stop seeing these needs as contradictory. Instead, you can create flexible frameworks that satisfy both drives. Maybe you plan pizza Friday but rotate different restaurants. Or you schedule "spontaneous time" where you decide in the moment what to do.

Your unique brain in love: How 50-70% co-occurrence changes everything

Medical research confirms what many people experience: autism and ADHD frequently occur together. But statistics don't capture the lived reality of loving someone when your brain processes connection through both conditions simultaneously.

Your autism might make you incredibly loyal and devoted to your partner. You form deep, lasting attachments and can focus intensely on your relationship. Meanwhile, your ADHD might make you easily distracted during conversations or impulsively reactive during conflicts. These traits create relationship dynamics that don't fit typical patterns.

Take Jennifer, a 26-year-old graphic designer: "I'm the most devoted girlfriend you'll ever meet. When I love someone, they become my special interest. I remember everything about them, notice tiny changes in their mood, and want to spend hours talking about our relationship. But I also interrupt them constantly, forget important dates despite caring deeply, and sometimes need to leave the room mid-conversation because I can't sit still."

Jennifer's experience shows how AuDHD creates unique relationship strengths alongside specific challenges:

Unique strengths:

- Deep, focused love and attention when your partner becomes a special interest
- Honest, direct communication that cuts through social games
- Creative problem-solving when relationship issues arise

- Intense emotional experiences that create powerful bonding
- Ability to hyperfocus on your partner's needs and interests

Specific challenges:

- Processing time differences that affect real-time communication
- Sensory needs that impact physical and emotional intimacy
- Executive function difficulties that affect relationship maintenance
- Emotional regulation differences during conflicts or stress

The exhaustion equation: Why relationships feel harder for you

Relationships require enormous amounts of mental energy for everyone. For you, the energy demands multiply because your brain processes social connection through two complex neurological systems simultaneously.

Your autism requires energy for social masking, processing nonverbal cues, and managing sensory input during interactions. Your ADHD demands energy for focus regulation, impulse control, and working memory management. Combine these with typical relationship maintenance tasks, and you're running multiple programs simultaneously.

Dr. Michelle Garcia Winner's research on social thinking explains how neurotypical brains automatically process social information. Your brain works harder because these processes aren't automatic. You're consciously managing what others do unconsciously, then adding ADHD's executive function challenges on top.

Consider David, a 31-year-old software developer: "After work, I have maybe two hours of social energy left. My girlfriend wants to talk about our days, plan weekend activities, and discuss relationship stuff. I want to connect with her, but my brain feels like a phone at

5% battery. If I force conversations when I'm depleted, I get snappy or zone out completely. Then she thinks I don't care."

David's experience illustrates the exhaustion equation:

Autism energy drains:

- Processing nonverbal communication
- Managing sensory input during conversations
- Translating emotions into words
- Maintaining eye contact and appropriate body language

ADHD energy drains:

- Sustaining attention during long conversations
- Inhibiting interrupting impulses
- Managing time awareness during interactions
- Filtering distracting thoughts or environmental stimuli

Combined effect:

- Faster depletion of social energy reserves
- Need for more recovery time between social interactions
- Higher likelihood of shutdown or meltdown when overstimulated
- Difficulty maintaining consistent energy for relationship maintenance

Internal trait conflicts: When your autism and ADHD disagree

The most confusing aspect of AuDHD relationships happens when your autism and ADHD traits pull you in opposite directions simultaneously. You might experience this as feeling torn between conflicting needs or never being able to satisfy both parts of yourself.

These conflicts show up in specific relationship situations:

Communication conflicts: Your autism wants time to process and respond thoughtfully. Your ADHD wants to respond immediately and interrupt with thoughts. Result: You either speak impulsively and regret it, or take so long to respond that conversations stall.

Social energy conflicts: Your autism needs alone time to recharge after social interaction. Your ADHD craves stimulation and connection. Result: You feel lonely but can't handle more social contact, or you push through social exhaustion and crash later.

Planning conflicts: Your autism wants detailed plans and predictable schedules. Your ADHD rebels against structure and craves flexibility. Result: You make plans that stress you out, or avoid planning and feel anxious about uncertainty.

Emotional expression conflicts: Your autism processes emotions slowly and carefully. Your ADHD feels emotions intensely and wants immediate expression. Result: You either suppress emotions until they explode, or express them before you understand what you're feeling.

Take Rachel, a 29-year-old nurse: "My boyfriend asks what I want for dinner. My autism brain immediately starts categorizing options by nutrition, budget, and preparation time. My ADHD brain screams 'TACOS!' without any reasoning. Then I get stuck because I can't decide if I want the logical choice or the impulsive choice. He's standing there waiting while I have an internal argument with myself."

Finding your baseline: What's neurodivergence vs. trauma vs. relationship issues

Separating typical AuDHD traits from trauma responses or relationship problems requires careful attention to patterns. Many experiences that look like relationship dysfunction actually stem from neurological differences that need accommodation rather than fixing.

Typical AuDHD traits in relationships:

- Needing processing time before responding to emotional conversations
- Experiencing sensory overwhelm during physical intimacy
- Having intense special interests that temporarily consume attention
- Requiring alone time to recharge after social interaction
- Struggling with executive function tasks like remembering dates or managing schedules

Potential trauma responses:

- Extreme fear of abandonment that persists despite partner reassurance
- Inability to trust partner's intentions even with consistent positive behavior
- Hypervigilance about partner's mood changes or facial expressions
- Dissociation during emotional conversations or physical intimacy
- Panic responses to normal relationship conflicts or disagreements

Relationship dysfunction:

- Partner dismissing or mocking your neurological needs
- Feeling forced to mask constantly with no space for authenticity
- Partner using your traits against you during arguments
- Lack of accommodation for your processing or sensory differences
- Feeling unsafe to express your actual thoughts or feelings

Lisa, a 32-year-old accountant, learned to distinguish these categories: "I used to think needing two hours to process an argument meant something was wrong with our relationship. But that's just how my brain works. What was wrong was my ex-boyfriend getting angry that I needed processing time. My current partner understands that I think better with time, so he'll say 'Let's table this and come back to it tomorrow.' That's accommodation, not dysfunction."

Practical Exercises and Tools

AuDHD Relationship Trait Mapper

Create a visual map of how your traits show up in relationships:

1. **Draw two overlapping circles** - label one "Autism traits" and one "ADHD traits"
2. **List autism traits in relationships:** deep loyalty, need for routine, sensory sensitivities, processing time needs, intense interests
3. **List ADHD traits in relationships:** impulsivity, distractibility, need for stimulation, emotional intensity, time blindness
4. **Identify overlapping traits:** rejection sensitivity, executive function challenges, emotional regulation differences
5. **Note conflict areas:** Where your autism and ADHD traits disagree
6. **Identify strengths:** How your unique combination creates relationship benefits

"My Conflicting Needs" Worksheet

For each conflict situation, identify both needs and brainstorm solutions:

Conflict: I need routine AND novelty

- **Autism need:** Predictable patterns for emotional safety
- **ADHD need:** Variety and stimulation to maintain interest
- **Solutions:** Flexible routines, planned spontaneity, rotating familiar activities

Conflict: I need processing time AND immediate response

- **Autism need:** Time to think through complex emotional topics
- **ADHD need:** Express thoughts before forgetting them

- **Solutions:** Voice memos to capture thoughts, scheduled follow-up conversations, note-taking during discussions

Self-Compassion Meditation for Racing/Rigid Thoughts

1. **Find a comfortable position** and set a 5-10 minute timer
2. **Acknowledge your thoughts:** "I notice my mind racing/getting stuck"
3. **Name your experience:** "This is what AuDHD feels like right now"
4. **Offer yourself kindness:** "My brain works differently, and that's okay"
5. **Use grounding phrases:** "I can hold space for both my autism and ADHD needs"

Quick Wins When Your Brain Fights Itself

For communication conflicts:

- Use the "pause and voice memo" technique—record your immediate thoughts, then listen and respond thoughtfully
- Create conversation scripts for common scenarios
- Practice the phrase: "I need a moment to process this"

For planning conflicts:

- Build flexibility into routines (same activity, different locations)
- Use "minimum viable plans" with room for spontaneous additions
- Schedule "chaos time" for unstructured activities

For energy conflicts:

- Track your energy patterns to identify optimal connection times
- Create "low-energy connection" options like watching movies together

- Communicate energy levels using a simple 1-10 scale

For emotional conflicts:

- Use emotion wheels to identify feelings quickly
- Practice delayed emotional expression: "I'm feeling something big, let me figure out what"
- Create emotional safety protocols for intense moments

Making Sense of Your Love Brain

AuDHD in relationships isn't a problem to solve—it's a unique way of experiencing love that requires specific understanding and accommodation. Your brain's complexity creates both challenges and extraordinary capacity for deep, authentic connection.

The key lies not in choosing between your autism and ADHD needs, but in finding creative ways to honor both. This might mean planning spontaneous adventures, creating flexible routines, or building relationships that can hold space for your full neurological reality.

Your love story won't look like neurotypical examples, and that's exactly as it should be. AuDHD brings intensity, creativity, loyalty, and authenticity to relationships that can create profound connections when both partners understand and work with your unique wiring.

Key Insights

- AuDHD creates unique relationship experiences beyond simple autism plus ADHD traits
- Internal conflicts between autism and ADHD needs require creative solutions, not choosing sides
- Relationship exhaustion comes from processing social connection through two complex neurological systems
- Distinguishing neurological traits from trauma or dysfunction helps you seek appropriate support
- Self-compassion for your conflicting needs is the foundation for healthy relationships

Chapter 2: The vulnerability factor no one talks about

The statistics hit like cold water: adults with ADHD and autism face significantly higher rates of relationship abuse and manipulation. Research from domestic violence organizations shows that neurodivergent individuals experience abuse at rates nearly three times higher than the general population. But numbers don't capture the daily reality of why this happens—or more importantly, how you can protect yourself.

Your AuDHD brain processes relationships differently. You might miss subtle warning signs that neurotypical people catch intuitively. You may struggle with pattern recognition in social situations. Your executive function differences can make it harder to track concerning behaviors over time. These aren't character flaws—they're neurological differences that create specific vulnerabilities.

Understanding these vulnerabilities isn't about fear-mongering or suggesting you can't have healthy relationships. You absolutely can. But knowledge is protection. Learning how your unique brain processes relationships helps you recognize when something isn't right and take action to keep yourself safe.

The perfect storm: Executive function + social differences = increased vulnerability

Your brain manages relationships through systems that work differently from neurotypical expectations. Executive function challenges affect your ability to track patterns, organize information about relationships, and plan responses to concerning situations. Social processing differences mean you might interpret behaviors differently than intended.

These differences combine to create vulnerability in specific ways:

Memory and pattern tracking difficulties make it harder to connect concerning behaviors across time. You might notice individual incidents but struggle to see the overall pattern. This is particularly challenging because manipulative people often space out concerning behaviors, making patterns harder to detect.

Social interpretation challenges can lead to misreading intentions or giving too much benefit of the doubt. Your tendency toward literal thinking might make you accept explanations that sound reasonable on the surface but don't account for underlying manipulation.

Executive function overload during relationship stress can impair your decision-making abilities. High stress situations can shut down your analytical thinking, making you more likely to react emotionally rather than logically assess the situation.

Consider Maria, a 29-year-old nurse with AuDHD who dated someone for eight months before recognizing the manipulation pattern: "He would criticize my 'weird' behaviors, then later say he was just trying to help me be more normal. Each incident seemed reasonable when he explained it. I have terrible working memory, so I couldn't hold all the incidents together in my mind to see the pattern. I started keeping a journal, and only then did I realize he was systematically breaking down my confidence in my own perceptions."

Maria's experience demonstrates how executive function challenges can mask patterns of psychological manipulation. Her difficulty with working memory—a common ADHD trait—made it impossible to track the accumulation of incidents. Without external memory aids like journaling, she couldn't see what was happening.

Trust Your Gut (Even When It's Complicated)

Your intuition works differently than neurotypical gut feelings. You might not get clear "this feels wrong" signals. Instead, watch for:

- Increased stimming or self-soothing behaviors around someone
- Feeling more tired after spending time with them

- Needing more recovery time after interactions
- Difficulty focusing during or after conversations
- Physical tension or discomfort in their presence

Why we miss red flags: Pattern recognition challenges in relationships

Red flag recognition depends on pattern identification across time and contexts. Your AuDHD brain might excel at recognizing patterns in areas of special interest but struggle with social pattern recognition, especially under stress or emotional intensity.

Traditional red flag lists often focus on dramatic behaviors that are easy to spot. But manipulation usually starts subtly. The person might begin by testing your boundaries in small ways, gradually escalating over time. This gradual escalation exploits your pattern recognition challenges.

Common early manipulation tactics that AuDHD individuals might miss:

Isolation disguised as special attention: "I love spending time just with you. Your friends don't really understand you like I do." This feels positive initially because it appears to value your uniqueness. But it gradually separates you from support systems.

Criticism disguised as helpfulness: "I'm telling you this because I care about you, but you need to work on making eye contact more. It makes people uncomfortable." This exploits your existing insecurities about social skills.

Control disguised as care: "You seem overwhelmed when you have to make decisions. I'll just handle our social calendar so you don't stress about it." This removes your agency while appearing considerate.

Take James, a 32-year-old teacher who didn't recognize escalating control: "My ex started by 'helping' me with social situations because

I find them draining. She'd answer for me at restaurants, decline social invitations on my behalf, and manage our schedule. I thought she was being caring because social stuff is hard for me. I didn't realize she was gradually taking control of all our decisions until I wanted to visit my sister and she got angry that I'd made plans without consulting her."

James's executive function challenges made it difficult to track how his autonomy was being systematically removed. Each individual incident seemed caring, but the pattern showed increasing control.

Specific red flags for AuDHD individuals:

Mocking or dismissing your neurological needs: Comments like "you're being too sensitive" or "that's not normal" about your sensory needs, processing time, or other AuDHD traits.

Using your traits against you: Bringing up your memory issues during arguments, claiming you're "too emotional" because of your rejection sensitivity, or using your need for routine to control your behavior.

Love bombing that exploits your dopamine system: Excessive attention, gifts, or intensity that feels amazing initially but creates dependency and makes normal relationships feel boring by comparison.

Gaslighting about your perceptions: Claiming you misunderstood situations because of your social processing differences, or insisting your memory of events is wrong because of your ADHD.

The gaslighting trap: When memory issues meet manipulation

Gaslighting—making someone question their own memory and perceptions—is particularly effective against people with ADHD because memory challenges are already present. Manipulative people can exploit your existing uncertainty about your memory to make you doubt your entire experience of events.

Your ADHD might affect working memory, making it harder to hold details in mind during conversations. Your autism might make you focus intensely on specific details while missing broader context. These differences can be exploited by someone who wants to rewrite history.

Consider the experience of Alex, a 27-year-old graphic designer: "My ex would bring up conversations we supposedly had that I couldn't remember. He'd say things like 'We talked about this, you agreed, don't you remember?' I have terrible memory for conversations, so I'd usually believe him. Then he started claiming I'd agreed to things I would never agree to—like not seeing my friends or quitting activities I loved. I started recording our conversations on my phone, and that's when I realized he was making up entire discussions that never happened."

Alex's working memory challenges made him vulnerable to false memory implantation. By consistently claiming conversations happened that didn't occur, his ex exploited Alex's uncertainty about his own memory.

Gaslighting tactics that target ADHD memory issues:

Claiming conversations that never happened: "We discussed this last week, you said you were fine with it."

Rewriting your emotional responses: "You weren't upset about that, you were laughing."

Minimizing documented events: "That text doesn't say what you think it says" or "You're reading too much into it."

Exploiting time blindness: "That was months ago, why are you still upset?" about recent events, or "That just happened" about things from long ago.

Protection strategies for memory vulnerabilities:

1. **Keep a relationship journal** documenting significant conversations and your emotional responses
2. **Use voice memos** to record your thoughts immediately after important discussions
3. **Screenshot or save important text conversations** that contradict gaslighting attempts
4. **Trust your emotional memory** even when factual details are unclear—your feelings about interactions are valid data
5. **Seek reality checking from trusted friends** who can help you process confusing interactions

Love bombing and dopamine: Why intensity feels like acceptance

Love bombing—excessive attention, affection, and intensity early in relationships—can feel particularly compelling to AuDHD individuals. Your dopamine system responds strongly to novel, intense stimulation. After a lifetime of feeling misunderstood or rejected, sudden intense acceptance can feel like everything you've been missing.

The neurological basis makes this vulnerability understandable. ADHD brains often have lower baseline dopamine, making intense experiences more rewarding. Autism can create deep hunger for acceptance and understanding. Love bombing temporarily satisfies both needs simultaneously.

Sarah, a 31-year-old marketing manager, describes her experience: "He seemed to understand me completely from day one. He loved my weird interests, thought my stimming was cute, and wanted to spend every minute together. After years of feeling like too much for people, someone finally wanted all of me. I ignored that he was also isolating me from friends and making decisions for us. The intensity felt like love, but it was actually control."

Sarah's experience shows how love bombing exploits the AuDHD hunger for acceptance. The person seemed to embrace her neurological differences, which felt so rare and special that she overlooked controlling behaviors.

Why love bombing works on AuDHD brains:

Dopamine flooding: The intense attention creates neurochemical reward that can become addictive **Acceptance hunger:** After lifetime experiences of rejection, intense acceptance feels healing **Special interest focus:** The person becomes a hyperfocus, making it harder to see flaws or problems **Social inexperience:** Fewer relationship experiences mean less ability to recognize unhealthy intensity **Rejection sensitivity:** Fear of losing this "perfect" person makes you overlook red flags

Love bombing warning signs:

- Wanting to spend all available time together immediately
- Excessive gifts or grand gestures very early in dating
- Claiming deep understanding of you after brief acquaintance
- Pushing for quick commitment or exclusivity
- Becoming upset if you want space or time with others
- Intense emotional expressions that feel disproportionate to relationship length

Healthy intensity versus love bombing:

Healthy intense connection develops gradually, respects your autonomy, encourages your other relationships, and feels stable over time.

Love bombing feels overwhelming, pushes for immediate commitment, discourages outside relationships, and often alternates with periods of withdrawal or criticism.

Breaking the statistics: From 9/10 risk to empowered awareness

Research indicates that up to 90% of autistic women experience some form of sexual or relationship violence in their lifetime. These statistics feel overwhelming, but understanding why these numbers exist helps you take protective action.

The high rates don't reflect something wrong with you—they reflect a society that doesn't teach people to recognize neurodivergent vulnerabilities or protect neurodivergent individuals from exploitation. Predatory people specifically target those they perceive as vulnerable.

But awareness changes everything. Once you understand your specific vulnerabilities, you can compensate for them. You can build external systems to track patterns, develop support networks for reality checking, and create boundaries that protect your unique needs.

Consider the transformation in Rebecca's approach to dating after learning about AuDHD vulnerabilities: "I used to trust everyone immediately and assume good intentions. Now I have a dating checklist—literally a list I keep on my phone. Do they respect my need for processing time? Do they encourage my friendships? How do I feel after spending time with them? It's not romantic, but it keeps me safe. I've avoided two situations that my past self would have gotten trapped in."

Rebecca's systematic approach compensates for her natural tendency to trust without verification. By creating external structure for evaluation, she protects herself while still being open to connection.

Empowerment strategies for AuDHD dating safety:

Trust verification over intuition: Create checklists and external tracking systems for evaluating relationships **Slow down the pace:** Take time to observe patterns before making commitments **Maintain outside perspectives:** Regular check-ins with trusted friends about your relationships **Document concerning behaviors:** Keep records to help with pattern recognition **Set clear boundaries early:** Communicate your needs and observe how they're respected

Your protective factors: Strengths that keep you safe

Your AuDHD traits aren't only vulnerabilities—they're also sources of strength that can protect you in relationships. Learning to leverage these strengths creates a balanced approach to relationship safety.

Autism-related protective factors:

Loyalty and dedication mean you invest deeply in relationships, creating strong bonds with healthy partners **Pattern recognition abilities** in areas of interest can be applied to relationship analysis with practice **Direct communication style** cuts through manipulation attempts and demands honesty **Strong sense of justice** helps you recognize unfair treatment once you learn to trust your perceptions **Attention to detail** can catch inconsistencies in stories or behavior with conscious effort

ADHD-related protective factors:

Intuitive pattern recognition can catch red flags quickly when you're not second-guessing yourself **Hyperfocus abilities** allow deep analysis of relationship dynamics when directed appropriately **Emotional intensity** provides strong signals about relationship health if you learn to trust them **Novelty-seeking** can help you maintain independence and outside interests **Quick thinking** enables rapid response to unsafe situations once you recognize them

Combined AuDHD protective factors:

Authenticity hunger makes you value genuine connection over surface-level interaction **Rejection of social norms** means you're less likely to stay in relationships due to societal pressure **Independence needs** can protect against complete enmeshment in unhealthy relationships **Special interest focus** on understanding yourself helps you develop self-awareness **Community connections** with other neurodivergent people provide reality-checking support

Mark, a 35-year-old engineer, learned to use his strengths protectively: "I started treating dating like debugging code—my special interest. I look for inconsistencies, test responses to boundaries, and track patterns over time. My autism makes me good at systematic analysis once I decide to apply it to relationships. My ADHD gives me gut reactions that I've learned to trust. Together, they're pretty good protection when I use them intentionally."

Practical Tools and Assessments

Red Flag Recognition Guide for AuDHD

Create a personalized checklist based on your specific vulnerabilities:

Memory-related red flags:

- Claims about conversations you can't remember
- Stories that change details over time
- Dismissal of your emotional reactions as "wrong"
- Pressure to make decisions quickly without processing time

Social processing red flags:

- Mocking your social differences as "weird" or "abnormal"
- Isolation from friends or family "for your own good"
- Speaking for you in social situations without permission
- Dismissing your need for social recovery time

Executive function red flags:

- Taking over tasks you can handle independently
- Creating chaos then "rescuing" you from overwhelm
- Using your organizational challenges against you in arguments
- Preventing you from developing your own systems and supports

Personal Vulnerability Assessment

Rate your current protection level in each area:

Memory tracking: Do you have systems for documenting important relationship events and conversations? **Pattern recognition:** Can you identify concerning behavior patterns over time? **Boundary setting:** Do you communicate your needs clearly and consistently? **Support network:** Do you have trusted people for reality-checking relationship concerns? **Self-advocacy:** Can you stand up for yourself during conflicts or disagreements?

Reality Check Journal Template

Daily relationship tracking format:

Date and situation: What happened today in my relationship? **My immediate emotional response:** How did I feel during and immediately after? **Partner's behavior:** What specific actions or words stood out? **My needs:** Were my neurological needs respected or dismissed? **Energy level:** Did this interaction drain or energize me? **Pattern notes:** Does this connect to anything I've noticed before?

Building Your Safety Foundation

Understanding vulnerability isn't about living in fear—it's about building awareness that protects you while still allowing genuine connection. Your AuDHD brain processes relationships differently, and that difference requires specific protective strategies.

The goal isn't to become suspicious of everyone or avoid relationships entirely. The goal is to develop conscious competence in relationship evaluation. You can learn to compensate for your natural vulnerabilities while building on your inherent strengths.

Safety in relationships comes from understanding yourself, trusting your perceptions (even when they're different from others'), and building systems that support your unique way of processing social connections. You deserve relationships that celebrate your authentic self while respecting your neurological needs.

Moving Forward with Confidence

Your path to healthy relationships starts with self-knowledge. Understanding your vulnerabilities helps you protect against them. Recognizing your strengths helps you build on them. Creating external systems helps you navigate areas where your brain needs support.

This awareness transforms you from someone who might be targeted for your differences into someone who understands and protects those same differences. You're not broken or incapable of healthy relationships—you just need different strategies than neurotypical dating advice provides.

The next step involves understanding another crucial aspect of AuDHD relationships: rejection sensitivity. Learning to manage the intense fear of being "too much" for others while still allowing authentic connection is essential for building the safe, genuine relationships you deserve.

Essential Takeaways

- AuDHD creates specific vulnerabilities in relationships through executive function and social processing differences
- Memory challenges can be exploited through gaslighting, but documentation systems provide protection
- Love bombing exploits dopamine systems and acceptance hunger, making intensity feel like love
- Your AuDHD traits include protective strengths that can be developed and used intentionally
- Awareness and systematic approaches to relationship evaluation transform vulnerability into empowerment

Chapter 3: Rejection sensitivity and the fear of being "too much"

The text message sits unread for three hours. Your heart pounds. Your mind spirals through every possible reason why your partner hasn't responded. Maybe they're finally tired of your questions about weekend plans. Maybe your need for reassurance yesterday was too much. Maybe they're realizing you're not worth the effort.

This is rejection sensitive dysphoria—a neurological reality that affects up to 99% of people with ADHD and frequently co-occurs with autism. It's not just sensitivity to rejection; it's an intense, overwhelming response to even perceived rejection that can shut down your entire nervous system.

RSD transforms normal relationship interactions into emotional minefields. A delayed text response becomes evidence of abandonment. A partner's tired expression becomes proof they find you annoying. Your brain interprets neutral or ambiguous social cues as rejection, creating a constant state of hypervigilance that exhausts both you and your relationships.

Understanding RSD changes everything about how you approach relationships. Once you recognize this neurological reality, you can develop strategies to manage it instead of being controlled by it.

RSD decoded: Why 98-99% of us experience this intensity

Rejection sensitive dysphoria isn't emotional immaturity or neediness—it's a neurological response pattern linked to ADHD brain structure and autism's intense emotional processing. Research from the Cleveland Clinic and other medical institutions confirms that RSD affects nearly all individuals with ADHD, with additional intensity often present in those who also have autism.

The neurological basis helps explain why RSD feels so overwhelming. Your brain processes social rejection through the same pain pathways as physical injury. For neurotypical people, this system provides important social feedback. For you, this system is hyperactive, triggering intense pain responses to minor social friction.

How RSD manifests neurologically:

Amygdala hyperactivation causes your threat detection system to interpret ambiguous social cues as rejection threats **Dopamine dysregulation** makes social acceptance feel more rewarding and rejection more devastating **Executive function shutdown** during RSD episodes impairs your ability to think logically about situations **Emotional flooding** overwhelms your capacity to regulate responses, leading to fight, flight, or freeze reactions

Consider Emma's experience as a 26-year-old therapist: "My girlfriend mentioned she needed some alone time after work. My logical brain knew this was normal—she's an introvert who recharges alone. But my RSD brain interpreted it as 'I'm too much, she's getting tired of me, this is the beginning of the end.' I spent the entire evening convinced our relationship was over because she needed two hours of quiet time."

Emma's response demonstrates classic RSD patterns. Her logical understanding couldn't override her neurological response to perceived rejection. The amygdala hijack created a cascade of catastrophic thinking that felt completely real and urgent.

RSD differs from typical rejection sensitivity in several ways:

Intensity level: RSD responses are disproportionately intense compared to the triggering situation **Physical manifestation:** Racing heart, difficulty breathing, nausea, or other physical symptoms **Duration:** Episodes can last hours or days rather than minutes **Functional impairment:** RSD can shut down your ability to think clearly or communicate effectively **Trigger sensitivity:** Even minor or ambiguous social cues can trigger intense responses

Common RSD triggers in relationships:

- Delayed responses to texts or calls
- Partner seeming distracted or preoccupied
- Changes in partner's routine or behavior
- Any form of constructive feedback or criticism
- Partner spending time with others
- Perceived tone changes in communication
- Cancelled plans or scheduling conflicts

The too-much paradox: Hiding yourself while craving connection

RSD creates a cruel paradox in relationships. You desperately want connection and acceptance, but you're terrified of being seen as "too much." This leads to hiding authentic parts of yourself, which prevents the genuine connection you crave.

The fear of being too much often stems from lifetime experiences of rejection for AuDHD traits. You've been told you're too sensitive, too intense, too demanding, or too weird. These messages create deep beliefs that your authentic self is unacceptable.

But hiding yourself creates relationships built on false foundations. Your partner falls for your masked version, not your real self. This makes you feel even more alone because you know they don't really know you.

Take David, a 30-year-old software developer: "I'm passionate about obscure programming languages—it's my special interest. But I learned to never talk about it because people's eyes glaze over. With my girlfriend, I pretend to be interested in mainstream stuff like sports and popular TV shows. She thinks we have so much in common, but she doesn't know the real me at all. I'm lonely even when we're together because I can't share what actually excites me."

David's experience shows how RSD fear leads to inauthentic relationships. His terror of being rejected for his real interests prevents genuine connection, creating the very loneliness he's trying to avoid.

The masking cycle in relationships:

1. **Fear of rejection** motivates hiding authentic traits
2. **Masking behaviors** create false persona
3. **Partner responds** to masked version
4. **Increased fear** of being discovered as "fraud"
5. **More intensive masking** to maintain false connection
6. **Burnout and resentment** from constant performance
7. **Relationship crisis** when mask becomes unsustainable

Breaking the too-much paradox requires:

Gradual authenticity: Slowly revealing real interests and traits rather than complete disclosure **Reality testing:** Checking whether your fears of being "too much" match actual partner responses **Self-compassion:** Treating your needs as valid rather than burdensome **Boundary setting:** Communicating your authentic needs clearly and consistently **Partner education:** Helping partners understand your neurological differences

When everything feels like rejection: Misreading partner cues

Your RSD brain interprets ambiguous social information through a rejection lens. Neutral expressions become annoyance. Distraction becomes disinterest. Tiredness becomes being tired of you. This creates a constant state of relationship anxiety that can damage otherwise healthy connections.

The misinterpretation happens automatically, below conscious awareness. Your brain fills in gaps in social information with rejection narratives because that's how it's learned to protect you from surprise rejection.

Common misinterpretations in RSD:

Facial expressions: Neutral faces appear angry or disappointed **Tone of voice:** Normal speaking tones sound irritated or distant

Response timing: Any delay in communication feels intentional and rejecting **Body language:** Normal positioning feels like withdrawal or avoidance **Attention patterns:** Normal distraction feels like deliberate ignoring **Mood changes:** Partner's bad days feel caused by your presence

Lisa, a 28-year-old teacher, describes her pattern: "My husband comes home from work looking tired, and I immediately assume I did something wrong. If he's quiet during dinner, I start reviewing everything I said or did that day to figure out what upset him. He's usually just processing his workday, but my brain can't accept that explanation. It has to be about me somehow."

Lisa's experience shows how RSD creates self-centered interpretations of others' behavior. Her brain can't hold space for her husband having experiences unrelated to their relationship.

Reality testing strategies for RSD misinterpretations:

Direct questioning: "You seem quiet tonight. Is everything okay with us, or are you processing other stuff?" **Assumption checking:** "I'm noticing I'm feeling anxious about your response time. Can you help me understand what's happening?" **Context consideration:** "What else might explain this behavior besides rejection of me?" **Pattern tracking:** "Does this person typically communicate this way, or is this unusual?" **Time delays:** "Let me wait an hour and see if I still interpret this the same way"

The people-pleasing trap: Losing yourself to avoid abandonment

RSD often drives people-pleasing behaviors as desperate attempts to prevent rejection. You might agree to things you don't want, suppress your opinions, or constantly seek reassurance. These behaviors temporarily reduce RSD anxiety but create long-term relationship problems.

People-pleasing prevents authentic relationships because your partner never learns your real preferences, boundaries, or needs. They can't truly know or love you if you're constantly shapeshifting to avoid their displeasure.

The tragedy of people-pleasing is that it often creates the very rejection you're trying to avoid. Partners may eventually feel frustrated by your lack of authenticity or exhausted by constant reassurance-seeking.

Consider Marcus, a 33-year-old nurse: "I said yes to everything my ex wanted. She liked hiking, so I pretended to love it despite hating being outdoors. She preferred staying home, so I gave up social activities I enjoyed. I thought I was being a good boyfriend, but she eventually said she felt like she was dating a mirror, not a person. My attempts to avoid rejection caused the rejection I was afraid of."

Marcus learned that preventing rejection by eliminating yourself doesn't create lasting connection. His ex ultimately rejected the empty version of himself he'd created to please her.

Common people-pleasing patterns in RSD:

Automatic agreement: Saying yes before considering your actual preferences **Opinion suppression:** Avoiding expressing views that might create conflict **Emotional caretaking:** Taking responsibility for partner's feelings and moods **Reassurance seeking:** Constantly asking if everything is okay or if they still like you **Conflict avoidance:** Suppressing your needs to prevent disagreements **Over-giving:** Excessive gifts, favors, or attention to secure attachment

Replacing people-pleasing with authentic relating:

Pause before agreeing: "Let me think about that and get back to you" **Express preferences:** "I'd prefer to do X, but I'm open to discussing alternatives" **Share opinions:** "I see it differently. Here's my perspective..." **Set boundaries:** "I'm not comfortable with that" or "That doesn't work for me" **Ask for needs:** "I need reassurance right now" instead of seeking it indirectly

Breaking the silence: Why we don't ask for what we need

RSD creates a cruel catch-22 around asking for support. You desperately need reassurance and understanding, but asking for these things feels risky because it reveals your vulnerability. What if your partner thinks you're needy? What if they get tired of providing reassurance?

This silence prevents partners from understanding your experience or learning how to support you effectively. They can't read your mind, and your attempts to hide your struggles leave them confused about your behavior.

Breaking the silence requires courage, but it's essential for authentic relationships. Partners who care about you want to understand your experience and support you appropriately.

Why AuDHD individuals avoid asking for RSD support:

Fear of being seen as needy: Believing your emotional needs are excessive or unreasonable **Shame about neurological differences:** Feeling defective for experiencing emotions differently **Past negative responses:** Previous partners who mocked or dismissed your sensitivity **Perfectionism:** Believing you should handle everything independently **Misreading social cues:** Interpreting partner's expressions as annoyance when asking for support

Sarah, a 31-year-old artist, learned to communicate her RSD needs: "I used to suffer in silence when my anxiety spiked. My partner would notice I was upset but not know why or how to help. Now I say things like 'My RSD is acting up about your delayed text response. I know logically you were in a meeting, but my brain is convinced you're mad at me. Can you help me reality-check this?' It feels vulnerable, but it actually makes our relationship stronger."

Sarah's approach demonstrates effective RSD communication. She names the experience, acknowledges the logical reality, and asks for specific support.

Scripts for asking for RSD support:

For reassurance: "I'm having an RSD moment where I'm convinced you're upset with me. Can you tell me we're okay?" **For reality checking:** "My brain is telling me your tone means you're annoyed with me. Is that accurate?" **For processing time:** "I'm feeling really sensitive right now. Can we revisit this conversation tomorrow?" **For understanding:** "When you seem distracted, my RSD interprets it as rejection. Can you help me understand what's actually happening?"

From reactive to responsive: Building RSD resilience

RSD recovery doesn't mean eliminating sensitivity—it means developing tools to manage intense responses so they don't control your relationships. You can learn to pause between trigger and reaction, creating space for logical thinking alongside emotional processing.

Building RSD resilience requires both in-the-moment tools and long-term strategies. You need immediate techniques for managing acute episodes and ongoing practices for reducing overall sensitivity.

In-the-moment RSD management:

Physical grounding: Focus on breath, feet on floor, or other sensory anchors **Reality testing questions:** "What evidence supports my interpretation? What evidence contradicts it?" **Time delays:** "I'll revisit this in an hour/tomorrow when I'm less activated" **Self-soothing:** Use stim toys, comfort objects, or calming activities **Communication:** "I'm having an RSD response right now and need some time to process"

Long-term RSD resilience building:

Pattern awareness: Track your RSD triggers and responses to identify patterns **Cognitive restructuring:** Practice alternative interpretations of ambiguous social cues **Self-compassion:** Treat yourself with kindness during RSD episodes **Nervous system

regulation: Regular practices that support emotional stability
Relationship security: Build evidence base of partner's consistent care and commitment

Michael, a 29-year-old chef, developed his RSD toolkit: "I have a note in my phone with reality-testing questions. I set a timer when I'm spinning out about rejection so I don't impulsively text my boyfriend for reassurance. I practice self-compassion phrases like 'This feeling is temporary and doesn't reflect reality.' It's taken months of practice, but I can usually catch RSD responses before they take over completely."

Practical Tools for RSD Management

RSD Emergency Kit Creation Guide

Physical items for regulation:

- Stress ball or fidget toy
- Comfortable headphones or earplugs
- Soft blanket or clothing item
- Photos of positive memories with partner
- Written reminder cards with reality-testing questions

Digital tools:

- Calming music playlist
- Voice memos from partner expressing love
- Screenshots of positive text conversations
- Meditation or breathing apps
- Journal app for tracking patterns

Reality-Testing Questions Card Deck

Create cards with these questions to use during RSD episodes:

Evidence checking:

- What concrete evidence supports my interpretation?
- What other explanations could account for this behavior?
- How has my partner typically responded in similar situations?
- Am I feeling rejected because of facts or feelings?

Context consideration:

- What else is happening in my partner's life right now?
- How am I feeling physically? (Hungry, tired, overwhelmed?)
- Have I been more sensitive lately due to stress or changes?
- Does this pattern match my partner's usual behavior?

Relationship security:

- How has my partner shown love and commitment recently?
- What evidence do I have that they enjoy my company?
- When have they chosen to spend time with me?
- How do they respond when I share vulnerabilities?

Partner Conversation Scripts for RSD Moments

For immediate episodes: "I'm having an RSD response right now where I'm interpreting [specific situation] as rejection. I know logically that might not be accurate, but my nervous system is activated. Can you help me reality-check this?"

For ongoing patterns: "I've noticed I get really anxious about rejection in our relationship, especially around [specific triggers]. This isn't about you doing anything wrong—it's how my brain works. Can we talk about ways you can support me when this happens?"

For requesting reassurance: "My rejection sensitivity is acting up today. I know you love me, but could you remind me? It helps my nervous system settle when I hear it directly."

For setting boundaries during episodes: "I'm too activated by rejection fears to have this conversation productively right now. Can we pause and come back to it tomorrow? I'm not avoiding the topic—I just need time to regulate."

RSD First Aid: What to Do in the Moment

Step 1: Recognize the response Notice physical sensations (racing heart, tight chest, nausea) and emotional flooding that signals RSD activation.

Step 2: Create safety Remove yourself from the triggering situation if possible. Go to a quiet space where you can regulate.

Step 3: Ground your nervous system Use breathing techniques, cold water on face, or physical movement to activate your parasympathetic nervous system.

Step 4: Reality test gently Ask yourself basic questions about evidence and alternative explanations, but don't force logical thinking if you're too activated.

Step 5: Seek appropriate support Reach out to partner, friend, or therapist for reality checking or comfort—but communicate that you're having an RSD response.

Step 6: Practice self-compassion Remind yourself that RSD is neurological, not a character flaw. You're doing your best with a challenging brain difference.

Understanding Your Unique Rejection Story

RSD affects everyone differently based on personal history, trauma experiences, and individual neurological patterns. Understanding your specific RSD profile helps you develop targeted strategies.

Your rejection story includes:

- **Early experiences** of criticism or rejection for AuDHD traits
- **Family patterns** around emotional expression and acceptance
- **School experiences** with peers and academic rejection
- **Previous relationships** and how they handled your sensitivity

- **Current stress levels** and life circumstances affecting your resilience

This understanding helps you recognize that RSD isn't random—it's your nervous system trying to protect you based on past experiences. While the responses may be disproportionate now, they made sense given your history.

Healing happens not through eliminating sensitivity, but through building security in current relationships and developing tools to manage intense responses. You can learn to honor your sensitivity while not being controlled by it.

The Path Beyond Fear

RSD will likely always be part of your relationship experience, but it doesn't have to dominate it. With understanding, tools, and practice, you can learn to surf the waves of rejection sensitivity rather than being overwhelmed by them.

The goal isn't to become someone who doesn't care about rejection—that would eliminate your capacity for deep connection and loyalty. The goal is to develop enough security and regulation skills that you can experience rejection fears without being controlled by them.

Your sensitivity, when managed well, can actually be a relationship strength. It helps you notice subtle relationship dynamics, motivates you to care for your connections, and creates capacity for deep emotional intimacy. The key is learning to trust yourself and your partner enough to weather the storms of RSD together.

As you build these skills, you'll naturally move toward the next crucial aspect of AuDHD relationships: learning to unmask safely with your partner. RSD often drives masking behaviors, so managing rejection sensitivity is essential groundwork for authentic intimacy.

Core Insights for RSD Management

- RSD is a neurological reality affecting 98-99% of people with ADHD, not emotional immaturity
- People-pleasing behaviors aimed at preventing rejection often create the rejection you fear
- Direct communication about RSD needs strengthens relationships rather than burdening them
- Reality-testing tools help distinguish between RSD responses and actual relationship problems
- Building RSD resilience takes time and practice but transforms your capacity for authentic connection

Chapter 4: Unmasking your way to real intimacy

The exhaustion hits you on Tuesday afternoon. You've been dating Alex for six months, and they think you're this easy-going, socially smooth person who loves spontaneous plans and crowded restaurants. But you're dying inside. Your real self—the one who needs three days' notice for social events and gets overwhelmed by restaurant noise—feels buried under layers of performance.

This is the masking paradox in relationships. You hide your authentic self to be lovable, but then feel unloved because no one knows who you really are. Your partner falls for a version of you that doesn't actually exist, leaving you feeling isolated even in a close relationship.

Masking in relationships isn't just autism masking or ADHD masking—it's both simultaneously. You're suppressing stimming while also forcing focus. You're hiding sensory needs while managing hyperactivity. You're performing neurotypical social skills while constantly monitoring for ADHD mistakes. The cognitive load becomes unsustainable.

The path to authentic intimacy requires gradually unmasking with your partner—revealing your real needs, struggles, and ways of being. This process feels terrifying because it risks rejection, but it's the only way to build relationships based on who you actually are rather than who you think you should be.

The masking toll: Why hiding both conditions exhausts you

Most people understand masking as hiding autism traits to appear more socially acceptable. But AuDHD masking is exponentially more complex because you're managing two different sets of neurological differences simultaneously, often with conflicting demands.

Your autism masking might involve suppressing stimming, forcing eye contact, following social scripts, and managing sensory overwhelm without visible reactions. Your ADHD masking involves controlling impulsivity, maintaining attention in conversations, managing hyperactivity, and hiding forgetfulness or disorganization.

The cognitive load creates what researchers call "dual masking exhaustion"—your brain runs multiple masking programs simultaneously while also trying to engage authentically in relationships. This leaves little mental energy for genuine connection or emotional presence.

Consider Jessica, a 27-year-old social worker: "With my boyfriend, I'm constantly running three programs at once. I'm suppressing my need to stim because I don't want to seem weird. I'm forcing myself to maintain eye contact during serious conversations even though it's painful. And I'm desperately trying to follow what he's saying without getting distracted, while pretending I'm naturally good at listening. By the end of dates, I'm so exhausted I need two days to recover, but he thinks I'm this naturally social person."

Jessica's experience illustrates how dual masking creates relationship disconnection despite physical presence. She's so busy performing neurotypicality that she can't actually engage with her partner authentically.

Specific costs of dual masking in relationships:

Cognitive exhaustion leaves little energy for emotional intimacy or genuine conversation **Emotional suppression** prevents sharing your real feelings and reactions **Sensory overwhelm** from forcing yourself into uncomfortable environments without accommodation **Memory problems** from cognitive overload affecting your ability to remember relationship details **Personality distortion** creates a false self that doesn't reflect your actual interests or needs **Burnout cycles** lead to periods where you can't maintain the performance and withdraw completely

Physical manifestations of masking exhaustion:

- Headaches or migraines after social interaction
- Muscle tension from suppressing movement or maintaining unnatural postures
- Digestive issues from stress and sensory overwhelm
- Sleep disruption from processing the day's social performances
- Increased illness frequency from chronic stress on immune system
- Fatigue that rest doesn't resolve

The authenticity gap: When partners only know your mask

The cruelest aspect of masking in relationships is feeling lonely while with someone who claims to love you. They love your mask, not your authentic self. This creates an authenticity gap—the distance between who your partner thinks you are and who you actually are.

The authenticity gap grows larger over time as you maintain increasingly complex performances. Your partner develops expectations based on your masked behavior. They expect you to always be available for social events because you've never said no. They assume you love busy restaurants because you've never complained about the noise. They think you're naturally organized because you've hidden your ADHD struggles.

Eventually, the mask becomes a prison. You can't reveal your real needs without seeming like you've been lying. You can't ask for accommodations without explaining why you've never needed them before. The relationship feels built on false foundations.

Take Michael, a 32-year-old teacher: "My girlfriend loves how 'flexible and adventurous' I am because I've said yes to everything for two years. Surprise weekend trips, loud concerts, last-minute dinner parties with her friends. I've never told her that spontaneous plans give me severe anxiety or that crowds are sensory torture. Now she's planning our vacation around music festivals and extreme sports. I'm trapped because saying no now means admitting I've been pretending to be someone else this whole time."

Michael's situation demonstrates how masking creates relationship momentum in directions that move away from your authentic needs. His girlfriend's love feels conditional on maintaining a personality that isn't real.

Signs of authenticity gap in relationships:

Partner surprise at your "new" needs: "You never minded crowds before" when you ask for accommodation **Feeling misunderstood despite closeness:** Your partner knows facts about you but not your inner experience
Relationship decisions that don't fit you: Plans, living situations, or activities that ignore your real needs **Loneliness despite connection:** Feeling isolated even during intimate moments **Fear of disappointment:** Believing your partner will leave if they see your real self **Performance anxiety:** Constant worry about maintaining your masked persona

Gradual revelation: A step-by-step unmasking process

Unmasking in relationships requires strategic planning rather than sudden revelation. Dropping all masks simultaneously can overwhelm both you and your partner. A gradual process allows for adjustment, education, and trust-building at sustainable pace.

The key is testing your partner's response to small revelations before sharing bigger vulnerabilities. This helps you gauge their capacity for acceptance and gives them time to learn about neurodivergence without being overwhelmed.

Phase 1: Testing the waters (Weeks 1-4)

Start with low-risk disclosures that reveal minor differences:

- "I get a bit overwhelmed in really noisy places"

- "I need to check my calendar before making plans"
- "I process things better when I can take notes"
- "I have some sensory sensitivities around textures"

Watch their response carefully. Do they seem curious and accommodating, or dismissive and annoyed? Their reaction to small differences predicts how they'll handle bigger revelations.

Phase 2: Educational sharing (Weeks 4-8)

Begin sharing information about neurodivergence generally:

- Share articles about autism or ADHD that resonate with you
- Mention friends or family members who are neurodivergent
- Discuss neurodiversity as a positive variation rather than deficit
- Observe their attitudes toward neurological differences

This phase helps you understand their baseline knowledge and attitudes before making personal disclosures.

Phase 3: Personal connection (Weeks 8-12)

Start connecting general neurodivergence information to your own experiences:

- "I relate to this article about sensory sensitivity"
- "I've always wondered if I might be on the autism spectrum"
- "Some of these ADHD traits sound familiar"
- "I'm learning more about how my brain works"

This allows exploration without full diagnosis disclosure while gauging their support for your self-discovery process.

Phase 4: Direct disclosure (Weeks 12-16)

Share your actual diagnosis or strong suspicion:

- "I've been diagnosed with autism and ADHD"
- "I'm AuDHD, which explains a lot about how I experience the world"
- "I want to share something important about how my brain works"

Include education about what this means for your relationship and what support you need.

Phase 5: Authentic living (Ongoing)

Begin living authentically rather than masking:

- Stim when you need to
- Ask for sensory accommodations
- Communicate processing needs
- Set boundaries around social energy
- Share special interests enthusiastically

Safe disclosure strategies: Testing the waters wisely

Not every partner will respond positively to neurodivergent disclosure. Some people have prejudices against neurological differences. Others may seem accepting initially but become frustrated when they understand the real implications. Testing responses protects you from emotional damage while gathering information about relationship viability.

Green flag responses to early disclosures:

Curiosity rather than judgment: "Tell me more about what that's like for you" **Accommodation offers:** "How can I help make this easier?" **Research initiative:** They educate themselves about neurodivergence independently **Respect for differences:** They don't try to "fix" or change you **Practical support:** They adjust their behavior to support your needs **Advocacy:** They defend your needs to others when appropriate

Yellow flag responses requiring caution:

Minimizing: "Everyone's a little autistic" or "That's just being human" **Fixing attempts:** Suggestions for how you could be "more normal" **Inconsistent accommodation:** Sometimes supportive, sometimes frustrated **Educational burden:** Expecting you to constantly explain and justify your needs **Conditional acceptance:** "I love you despite your diagnosis"

Red flag responses indicating unsuitability:

Denial or dismissal: "You don't seem autistic" or "You're making excuses" **Mockery or ridicule:** Making fun of your traits or calling you "retarded" **Exploitation:** Using your vulnerabilities against you during conflicts **Isolation attempts:** Discouraging you from neurodivergent community or resources **Abuse:** Any form of physical, emotional, or psychological harm related to your neurodivergence

Rachel, a 29-year-old graphic designer, learned to test responses carefully: "I started by mentioning I needed quiet time to recharge after social events. My ex said 'That's antisocial, you need to push yourself more.' Red flag. My current partner said 'Of course, how much time do you usually need?' and started planning our social calendar with recovery time built in. Green flag. The difference taught me what acceptance actually looks like."

When to unmask vs. when to protect: Boundary navigation

Unmasking isn't always safe or appropriate. Some situations require strategic masking for your protection, employment, or social safety. Learning when to unmask versus when to protect yourself is a crucial skill for navigating an often neurodivergent-unfriendly world.

Situations where unmasking may be safe:

Long-term committed relationships where your partner has demonstrated consistent acceptance **Close friendships** with people who have shown genuine interest in understanding you **Neurodivergent-friendly environments** like support groups or understanding communities **Safe family relationships** where you have evidence of unconditional love **Professional settings** with accommodating policies and understanding supervisors

Situations requiring careful consideration:

New relationships where you haven't tested responses to differences yet **Work environments** where discrimination could affect your livelihood **Social situations** with people who have limited neurodivergence understanding **Family gatherings** with relatives who have history of judgment or criticism **Medical appointments** where providers might dismiss your concerns

Situations where masking may be protective:

Legal proceedings where being perceived as "different" could affect outcomes **Job interviews** in neurotypical organizations without diversity commitments **Emergency medical care** where advocating for yourself requires appearing "credible" **Confrontational situations** where vulnerability could be exploited **Unsafe social environments** where differences might trigger harassment

The goal isn't to unmask everywhere—it's to make conscious choices about when authenticity serves you versus when strategic masking protects you.

Consider Tom's approach as a 34-year-old accountant: "I'm fully unmasked with my wife and close friends. I'm partially unmasked at work—they know I'm autistic and need accommodations, but I still suppress stimming during client meetings. I mask completely with my in-laws because they've made it clear they don't 'believe' in neurodivergence. It's not ideal, but it's strategic. I pick my battles."

Rebuilding from burnout: Post-masking recovery in relationships

Chronic masking often leads to autistic burnout—a state of physical, emotional, and mental exhaustion that can last months or years. Recovery requires radical lifestyle changes, including major adjustments to how you show up in relationships.

Burnout recovery means you can't maintain previous levels of social performance. You might need more alone time, fewer social commitments, and extensive accommodations. This can strain relationships with partners who don't understand the severity of your situation.

Burnout symptoms affecting relationships:

Extreme social exhaustion making any interaction feel overwhelming **Sensory sensitivity increases** requiring environmental modifications **Executive function decline** affecting your ability to manage relationship tasks **Emotional dysregulation** causing stronger reactions to minor stresses **Communication difficulties** making it hard to express needs or feelings **Withdrawal tendencies** preferring isolation to social connection

Supporting relationship during burnout recovery:

Reduce social obligations to absolute minimum necessary **Increase sensory accommodations** in shared living spaces **Communicate energy levels** using simple scales or signals **Delegate relationship maintenance** tasks to partner temporarily **Lower performance expectations** for yourself and communicate this need **Prioritize rest and regulation** over relationship activities

Maria, a 31-year-old nurse, navigated burnout recovery with her husband: "I had to tell him that the person he married was mostly a performance, and I couldn't keep performing anymore. I needed six months of basically no social obligations, lots of alone time, and accommodation for sensory needs I'd been hiding for years. He was confused and hurt initially, but once he understood it was medical recovery, not rejection of him, he became incredibly supportive."

Maria's experience demonstrates how reframing burnout as medical recovery rather than relationship rejection helps partners understand the necessity of major lifestyle changes.

Practical Tools for Safe Unmasking

Masking Inventory Worksheet

Identify your current masking behaviors across different areas:

Social masking:

- Forcing eye contact during conversations
- Suppressing stimming or fidgeting
- Following neurotypical conversation scripts
- Hiding special interests or intense focus areas

Sensory masking:

- Tolerating uncomfortable environments without complaint
- Suppressing reactions to overwhelming input
- Wearing uncomfortable clothing for appearance
- Attending events despite sensory challenges

Executive function masking:

- Hiding organization struggles or memory issues
- Pretending to follow complex instructions easily
- Concealing time management difficulties
- Over-compensating for attention challenges

Emotional masking:

- Suppressing intense emotions or reactions
- Pretending to process feelings at neurotypical speed

- Hiding need for processing time or space
- Minimizing impact of rejection sensitivity

Gradual Unmasking Plan Template

Create a timeline for revealing authentic self:

Month 1: Foundation building

- Share general interest in neurodivergence
- Mention minor sensory preferences
- Introduce concept of different communication styles

Month 2: Education phase

- Share articles or videos about AuDHD
- Discuss neurodiversity as brain variation
- Gauge partner's attitudes and receptivity

Month 3: Personal connection

- Connect general information to your experiences
- Share childhood stories that make sense with AuDHD context
- Introduce possibility of your own neurodivergence

Month 4: Direct disclosure

- Share diagnosis or strong self-identification
- Provide education about what this means
- Discuss implications for relationship

Months 5-6: Authentic living

- Gradually reduce masking behaviors
- Implement needed accommodations
- Address partner questions and concerns

"My Authentic Self" Partner Sharing Guide

Structure for major disclosure conversation:

Opening: "I want to share something important about myself with you because I care about our relationship and want you to really know me."

Context: "I've learned that I'm AuDHD—both autistic and ADHD. This explains a lot about how I experience the world."

Education: "This means my brain processes [social situations/sensory input/emotions] differently than neurotypical people."

Personal impact: "For me, this shows up as [specific examples relevant to your relationship]."

Relationship implications: "I've been masking some of these traits because I was scared you'd find them weird or too much."

Needs: "What I need from you is [specific support requests]."

Questions: "What questions do you have? What would help you understand this better?"

Reassurance: "This doesn't change how I feel about you or our relationship. If anything, I'm sharing this because I want us to be closer."

Small Steps to Big Authenticity

Week 1-2: Sensory honesty

- "This restaurant is pretty loud for me"
- "I prefer textures that are [soft/smooth/etc.]"
- "Bright lights give me headaches"

Week 3-4: Communication needs

- "I process better when I can take notes"
- "I need a moment to think about that"
- "Can you repeat that? I got distracted"

Week 5-6: Social energy

- "I need some quiet time after social events"
- "I'm feeling a bit peopled out today"
- "Can we have a low-key evening?"

Week 7-8: Emotional processing

- "I need time to process my feelings about this"
- "I'm feeling overwhelmed and need to step back"
- "My emotions feel really intense right now"

Week 9-10: Special interests

- Share something you're genuinely passionate about
- Explain why certain topics fascinate you
- Ask if they want to learn about your interests

The Journey to Real Connection

Unmasking in relationships is simultaneously the most terrifying and most liberating thing you can do. The terror comes from risking rejection of your authentic self. The liberation comes from finally being known and loved for who you actually are.

Not every relationship will survive unmasking, and that's actually good information. Relationships that can only exist when you're performing aren't really relationships—they're ongoing auditions. You deserve to be loved for your real self, not for how well you can pretend to be someone else.

The process takes time, courage, and patience with both yourself and your partner. But the reward—authentic intimacy with someone who knows and accepts your full reality—is worth every difficult conversation and vulnerable moment.

As you practice unmasking, you'll discover that your authentic self is not only lovable but brings unique gifts to relationships. Your directness cuts through social games. Your intensity creates deep connections. Your different perspective offers fresh insights. Your loyalty and dedication create secure bonds.

The path forward involves building on this authentic foundation to develop communication skills that work with your AuDHD brain rather than against it. Learning to express your needs clearly and navigate conflicts honestly becomes much easier when you're no longer hiding who you are.

Foundations for Authentic Love

- Dual masking of autism and ADHD traits creates unsustainable cognitive load in relationships
- Gradual unmasking allows partners to adjust while you test their capacity for acceptance
- Strategic masking in unsafe situations protects you while full authenticity builds genuine intimacy
- Burnout recovery may require temporary relationship modifications but leads to stronger connections
- Your authentic self brings unique strengths to relationships that masking prevents partners from experiencing

Chapter 5: Communication when words are hard

Your partner asks a simple question: "How was your day?" But your ADHD brain is still processing seventeen different things that happened, while your autism brain wants to give a detailed, chronologically accurate account that includes every relevant detail. Meanwhile, your mouth blurts out "fine" because that's the socially expected response, even though your day was anything but fine.

This is the daily reality of AuDHD communication. Your autism wants precision, context, and time to process. Your ADHD wants to interrupt, jump between topics, and respond immediately before forgetting what you wanted to say. These conflicting needs create communication patterns that confuse both you and your partner.

The solution isn't learning to communicate like neurotypical people—it's developing communication systems that work with your unique brain rather than against it. This means creating new frameworks, tools, and approaches that honor both your autism and ADHD needs while building genuine connection with your partner.

The communication challenge: Autism precision meets ADHD impulsivity

Research from Psychology Today and the ADD Resource Center shows that both autism and ADHD significantly affect communication patterns, but in different ways. Autism typically involves careful processing, literal interpretation, and detailed expression. ADHD involves quick responses, topic jumping, and difficulty maintaining attention during long conversations.

Having both conditions creates internal communication conflicts that your partner can't see but definitely experiences. You might start answering their question with careful consideration, then suddenly interrupt yourself with a related thought, then forget your original point, then feel frustrated that you can't communicate clearly.

Consider David, a 32-year-old engineer: "My wife asks what I want for dinner. My autism brain immediately starts categorizing options by nutrition, cost, and preparation time. But my ADHD brain interrupts with 'PIZZA!' before I finish thinking. Then I start explaining why pizza might not be the best choice, but halfway through my explanation, I notice she looks frustrated, so I stop mid-sentence and ask if she's okay, which confuses her even more because now we're not talking about dinner anymore."

David's experience illustrates the collision between autism's systematic processing and ADHD's impulsive responding. His partner receives conflicting communication signals that seem inconsistent or confusing.

Common AuDHD communication patterns:

Start-stop-restart conversations where you begin topics, get distracted, then return to them later **Over-explaining followed by under-explaining** depending on which condition is driving the moment **Interrupting yourself** to add details or correct previous statements **Topic jumping** that makes logical sense to you but seems random to others **Processing delays** that create awkward silences while your brain catches up **Hyperfocus communication** where you talk extensively about special interests **Shutdown responses** when overwhelmed by communication demands

How partners experience AuDHD communication challenges:

Partners often feel confused by the apparent inconsistency in your communication style. Sometimes you're incredibly articulate and detailed. Other times you seem scattered or nonresponsive. They may interpret these differences as mood changes or relationship issues rather than neurological variations.

Sarah, whose partner has AuDHD, explains: "I never know which version of him I'm going to get in conversations. Sometimes he gives me these amazing, thoughtful responses that show he's really listened and processed what I said. Other times he interrupts me mid-sentence or gives one-word answers. I used to think he was mad at me or losing interest, but now I understand his brain just works differently on different days."

Alternative channels: When talking isn't working

Traditional relationship advice assumes that talking is the primary—and best—form of communication. But your AuDHD brain might process and express information better through alternative channels. Text messaging, written notes, voice recordings, or even shared documents can sometimes convey meaning more effectively than face-to-face conversation.

Why alternative channels work for AuDHD communication:

Processing time allows your autism brain to formulate clear, accurate responses **Reduced sensory load** from not managing eye contact, body language, and environmental stimuli simultaneously
Edit capability lets you refine your message before sending
Permanent record helps with ADHD memory challenges **Reduced interruption risk** since you can't physically interrupt written communication **Special interest accommodation** through sharing links, articles, or detailed explanations

Effective alternative communication methods:

Text messaging for daily logistics reduces the cognitive load of phone calls or in-person planning **Voice memos for emotional processing** allow you to work through feelings before discussion **Shared digital notes** for ongoing topics that need multiple conversations **Email for complex topics** that require detailed explanation or documentation **Visual aids** like charts or diagrams for abstract concepts **Written check-ins** using standardized formats that reduce communication barriers

Take Maria, a 29-year-old therapist: "My girlfriend and I do most of our serious relationship talks through shared Google docs. I know it sounds unromantic, but it works for us. I can process her concerns thoroughly and respond thoughtfully without my ADHD making me interrupt or my autism making me struggle with eye contact during emotional conversations. We've had deeper, more honest communication this way than we ever did sitting across from each other."

Maria's approach demonstrates how alternative channels can actually increase intimacy rather than reducing it. By removing barriers to clear communication, couples can focus on understanding rather than navigating neurological challenges.

Quick Scripts for Common Scenarios

When you need processing time: "I want to give you a thoughtful response to this. Can I text you my thoughts in an hour?"

When you're communication-overwhelmed: "I'm hitting my conversation limit for today. Can we pause and pick this up tomorrow?"

When you need to use alternative methods: "I communicate better in writing for emotional topics. Would you be open to texting about this?"

When you're hyperfocusing: "I realize I've been talking about my special interest for a while. What did you want to share?"

The pause protocol: Building processing time into conversations

Your autism brain needs time to process information and formulate responses, but your ADHD brain fears that pauses will lead to forgotten thoughts or lost conversation flow. Creating structured pause protocols helps both parts of your brain get what they need.

The pause protocol involves explicitly building processing time into conversations rather than expecting immediate responses. This reduces pressure on you while helping your partner understand that delays aren't disinterest or confusion.

Three types of pauses for AuDHD communication:

Micro-pauses (10-30 seconds) for simple question processing
Processing pauses (1-5 minutes) for emotional or complex topics
Extended pauses (hours to days) for major decisions or relationship discussions

How to implement pause protocols:

1. **Establish the system** by explaining your processing needs to your partner
2. **Use clear signals** like "pause please" or a hand gesture to indicate need for processing time
3. **Set time expectations** so your partner knows approximately how long you need
4. **Return to topics** proactively rather than hoping your partner will remember to ask again
5. **Express appreciation** for your partner's patience with your processing style

Jake, a 35-year-old teacher, developed his pause system: "I tell my husband 'processing pause' when I need time to think. For simple stuff, I hold up one finger for a minute. For bigger things, I say 'overnight pause' and we come back to it the next day. He used to think my silences meant I was upset or didn't care. Now he understands I'm actually working hard to give him a good response."

Sample pause protocol phrases:

For micro-pauses: "Give me just a second to think about that" **For processing pauses:** "I want to consider this carefully. Can I have five minutes?" **For extended pauses:** "This deserves a thoughtful response. Can we talk about it tomorrow evening?" **For returning to topics:** "I've been thinking about what you said yesterday, and here's my response"

Script library: Templates for difficult discussions

AuDHD brains often struggle with generating appropriate language during emotionally charged conversations. Your autism wants to be precise and honest, but your ADHD makes you impulsive or forgetful. Having pre-written scripts provides structure while allowing for personalization.

Essential scripts for AuDHD relationships:

Conflict de-escalation script: "I can see we're both upset right now. I care about resolving this, but I need to pause so I can communicate clearly instead of reactively. Can we come back to this in [timeframe] when we're both calmer?"

Sensory overwhelm script: "I'm getting sensory overload right now, which is affecting my ability to focus on our conversation. It's not about you or the topic—I just need to [reduce stimulation/take a break/change environments] so I can engage fully."

Processing needs script: "I want to give you a thoughtful response to this important topic. My brain needs time to process before I can communicate clearly. Can I [text you later/talk about this tomorrow/write down my thoughts] and then we can discuss?"

Misunderstanding repair script: "I think we're miscommunicating somehow. Can we both try rephrasing what we're trying to say? I want to make sure I understand you correctly and that you understand what I mean."

Need for clarity script: "I'm not sure I'm following everything you're saying. Could you help me understand by [repeating the main point/giving me a specific example/writing it down]? I want to respond appropriately."

Lisa, a 31-year-old nurse, uses scripts regularly: "I have standard phrases saved in my phone for common relationship situations. When my boyfriend and I start miscommunicating, I literally read from my script: 'I think we're talking past each other. Can we slow down and make sure we understand each other?' It might sound robotic, but it prevents arguments and actually leads to better communication."

Non-verbal options: Beyond words to connection

Not all communication needs to involve words. Your AuDHD brain might express and receive love more clearly through non-verbal channels that don't require the complex processing demands of spoken language.

Non-verbal communication strengths for AuDHD:

Physical presence without pressure to talk **Shared activities** that create connection through common focus **Written expressions** like notes, cards, or messages **Gift-giving** that shows attention to partner's interests **Service acts** that demonstrate care through actions **Artistic expression** through music, art, or creative projects

Practical non-verbal communication strategies:

Daily connection rituals like brief hugs or hand-holding that don't require conversation **Shared special interests** where you connect through common activities rather than talking about them **Comfort gestures** like bringing tea, adjusting lighting, or other environmental supports **Digital love languages** like sending articles, memes, or music that express your feelings **Parallel presence** where you're physically together but engaged in separate, comfortable activities

Consider Tom's approach as a 33-year-old programmer: "My wife and I do 'kitchen togetherness' most evenings. She cooks while I clean, and we're together but don't have to maintain conversation. Sometimes we talk, sometimes we don't, but we're connected. It's actually more intimate than forced dinner conversation because there's no pressure to perform socially."

Repair strategies: Fixing communication breakdowns

Communication breakdowns are inevitable in AuDHD relationships, but they don't have to damage your connection. Having clear repair strategies helps you address misunderstandings quickly before they create larger relationship problems.

The three-step AuDHD communication repair process:

Step 1: Recognize the breakdown Notice signs like confusion, frustration, or emotional escalation that indicate communication isn't working.

Step 2: Pause and reset Stop the current communication attempt and acknowledge that you need to try a different approach.

Step 3: Choose alternative method Switch to a communication channel or style that works better for the current situation.

Common breakdown patterns and repairs:

Pattern: Overwhelming detail vs. impatient listening **Repair:** "I'm giving you too much information at once. Let me start with the main point and you can ask for details if you want them."

Pattern: Impulsive interrupting vs. need for complete thoughts **Repair:** "I keep interrupting because I'm afraid I'll forget my thoughts. Can I jot down notes while you talk, then respond when you're finished?"

Pattern: Literal interpretation vs. implied meaning **Repair:** "I think I'm missing the underlying message here. Could you be more direct about what you need from me?"

Pattern: Emotional overwhelm vs. logical discussion **Repair:** "I'm too emotionally activated to think clearly right now. Can we pause this conversation and come back to it when I'm regulated?"

Practical Communication Tools

Communication Style Assessment for Both Partners

Each partner completes this assessment to understand communication preferences:

Processing style preferences:

- Do you prefer immediate responses or time to think?
- Do you communicate better verbally or in writing?
- Do you need environmental modifications for difficult conversations?
- How do you signal when you need processing time?

Conversation structure preferences:

- Do you prefer structured discussions or organic conversations?
- How do you handle interruptions or topic changes?
- What helps you stay focused during longer conversations?
- How do you prefer to address misunderstandings?

Emotional communication preferences:

- How do you express strong emotions effectively?
- What helps you stay regulated during difficult topics?
- How do you prefer to receive feedback or criticism?
- What does emotional support look like for you?

Customizable Script Templates

Create personalized versions of these templates:

For requesting communication accommodations: "I communicate best when [specific conditions]. Would it work for you if we [accommodation request]?"

For addressing misunderstandings: "I think we're not understanding each other. Could we try [alternative approach] to make sure we're on the same page?"

For managing emotional discussions: "This topic is emotionally challenging for me. I need [specific support] to have this conversation effectively."

"Weather Report" Daily Check-in System

Create a simple system for sharing daily communication capacity:

Green weather: Full communication capacity, available for complex discussions **Yellow weather:** Limited capacity, prefer simple conversations **Red weather:** Low capacity, need minimal communication demands **Storm warning:** Overwhelmed, need space and recovery time

Partners can share their daily "weather" to adjust communication expectations appropriately.

Building Your Communication Foundation

AuDHD communication requires patience, creativity, and willingness to do things differently than neurotypical relationship advice suggests. Your brain's unique combination of autism precision and ADHD spontaneity can actually create richer, more authentic communication—once you develop systems that work with your neurology rather than against it.

The goal isn't to eliminate all communication challenges—it's to develop tools and strategies that reduce friction while building genuine understanding between you and your partner. This foundation becomes especially crucial when addressing the next major aspect of AuDHD relationships: sensory needs and physical intimacy.

Effective communication sets the stage for discussing sensory boundaries, expressing physical needs, and creating intimate environments that work for your unique nervous system. The scripts and systems you develop here will support every other aspect of your relationship.

Essential Communication Frameworks

- AuDHD communication involves navigating conflicts between autism precision and ADHD impulsivity

- Alternative communication channels often work better than traditional face-to-face conversation
- Pause protocols build necessary processing time into discussions without losing conversation flow
- Script libraries provide structure for difficult conversations while allowing personalization
- Communication breakdowns are normal and repairable using systematic approaches

Chapter 6: Sensory intimacy and physical connection

The candlelit dinner your partner planned feels like sensory torture. The flickering light triggers visual sensitivity. The restaurant noise overwhelms your auditory processing. Your date's cologne smells too strong. The scratchy tablecloth bothers your tactile system. Meanwhile, your partner thinks they've created the perfect romantic setting and can't understand why you seem uncomfortable.

This disconnect between neurotypical intimacy expectations and AuDHD sensory realities affects every aspect of physical relationships. Your sensory needs aren't preferences or pickiness—they're neurological requirements for comfort and connection. But most relationship advice ignores sensory differences entirely, leaving you to figure out intimate connection on your own.

Understanding your sensory intimacy profile changes everything about how you approach physical relationships. Instead of forcing yourself to tolerate overwhelming environments or touch experiences, you can create intimate connections that actually feel good to your nervous system.

Your sensory intimacy profile: Beyond typical advice

Standard intimacy advice assumes everyone processes touch, sound, sight, smell, and taste the same way. Your AuDHD brain processes sensory information differently, which means typical romantic scripts often create discomfort rather than connection.

Your sensory profile includes both hypersensitivities (too much input) and hyposensitivities (not enough input) across different sensory systems. You might crave deep pressure touch while being overwhelmed by light touch. You might need complete silence while also craving certain types of music. These seeming contradictions make perfect sense once you understand how your individual nervous system works.

The eight sensory systems affecting intimacy:

Tactile (touch): Light touch, deep pressure, temperature, texture sensitivity **Auditory (hearing):** Volume sensitivity, sound processing, background noise tolerance **Visual (sight):** Light sensitivity, motion sensitivity, visual processing challenges **Olfactory (smell):** Scent sensitivity, perfume/cologne reactions, natural body odors **Gustatory (taste):** Food textures, flavors, oral sensitivity during kissing **Vestibular (balance/movement):** Motion sensitivity, position changes, spatial orientation **Proprioceptive (body awareness):** Joint compression, body position, movement coordination **Interoceptive (internal awareness):** Hunger, thirst, need for bathroom, arousal awareness

Consider Emma's sensory profile as a 28-year-old teacher: "I have tactile hypersensitivity for light touch but hyposensitivity for deep pressure. This means gentle caressing feels irritating or ticklish, but firm massage or tight hugs feel amazing. My ex thought I didn't like physical affection because I'd pull away from soft touches. My current partner learned to give me firm, consistent pressure instead, and now physical intimacy actually feels good instead of overwhelming."

Emma's experience demonstrates how understanding your specific sensory needs transforms intimate experiences from endurance tests into genuine pleasure.

Creating your sensory intimacy map:

Hypersensitivities (too much input):

- Which sensory inputs feel overwhelming or painful?
- What environments make physical intimacy difficult?
- Which types of touch feel irritating or uncomfortable?
- What sounds, smells, or lighting interfere with connection?

Hyposensitivities (not enough input):

- Which sensory inputs do you crave more of?
- What types of touch feel good and calming?

- Which environments help you feel more connected?
- What sensory experiences increase your arousal or interest?

Sensory supports:

- Which accommodations help you feel comfortable during intimacy?
- What environmental modifications improve your experience?
- Which sensory tools or aids support your needs?
- How can your partner provide helpful sensory input?

The environment equation: Setting the stage for connection

Your physical environment dramatically affects your capacity for intimacy and connection. Factors that neurotypical people might not even notice—like lighting type, background noise, room temperature, or fabric textures—can make the difference between feeling safe and connected versus overwhelmed and shut down.

Creating sensory-friendly intimate environments isn't about eliminating all stimulation—it's about optimizing your environment to support your nervous system's specific needs.

Key environmental factors for AuDHD intimacy:

Lighting considerations:

- Harsh fluorescent lights can trigger migraine or sensory overload
- Flickering candles might cause visual processing issues
- Complete darkness might increase anxiety or disorientation
- Adjustable lighting allows customization based on current needs

Sound environment:

- Background noise from traffic, neighbors, or appliances can be distracting
- Sudden sounds can trigger startle responses that interrupt intimacy
- Some people need complete silence while others need consistent white noise
- Music can be helpful or overwhelming depending on volume and type

Temperature and air quality:

- Overheating can cause sensory overwhelm and shutdown
- Cold environments might make physical touch uncomfortable
- Air circulation affects comfort and ability to focus
- Humidity levels impact sensory sensitivity

Texture and fabric considerations:

- Bedding materials affect comfort during physical intimacy
- Clothing textures can be distracting or irritating
- Room surfaces and decorations contribute to overall sensory experience
- Organization level affects some people's ability to relax

Take Marcus, a 34-year-old graphic designer: "My girlfriend and I spent months figuring out our bedroom environment. I need weighted blankets for deep pressure but can't handle flannel sheets because the texture is too much. She needs cool temperatures but I get cold easily. We finally found bamboo sheets that feel smooth to me, and we use separate blankets so she can be cool while I stay warm under my weighted blanket. It sounds complicated, but now our bedroom actually feels like a place where we can both be comfortable and intimate."

Marcus's trial-and-error process illustrates how environmental optimization requires experimentation and compromise, but results in dramatically improved intimate experiences.

Touch navigation: From aversion to preference mapping

Touch preferences in AuDHD relationships are complex and often misunderstood. You might enjoy certain types of touch while finding others overwhelming or irritating. Your touch needs might change based on your current sensory state, stress level, or time of day.

Understanding touch preferences prevents misinterpretation of your responses. When you pull away from light touch, you're not rejecting your partner—you're responding to sensory input that feels uncomfortable. When you crave firm pressure, you're not being demanding—you're seeking sensory input that helps your nervous system regulate.

Common AuDHD touch patterns:

Light touch sensitivity: Gentle caressing, tickling, or soft touches feel irritating rather than pleasant **Deep pressure seeking:** Firm hugs, massage, or weighted blankets feel calming and connecting **Temperature sensitivity:** Warm or cold touch might be overwhelming or particularly sought after **Texture preferences:** Smooth vs. rough skin, moisturized vs. dry hands, fabric vs. skin contact **Duration limits:** Some touches feel good briefly but become overwhelming if continued **Timing sensitivity:** Touch needs change based on current sensory state or emotional regulation

Touch mapping exercise:

Work with your partner to map your touch preferences:

Green touches (always welcome): List specific types of touch that consistently feel good **Yellow touches** (sometimes okay): Identify touches that depend on your current state **Red touches** (generally unwelcome): Note touches that typically feel overwhelming or irritating **Blue touches** (especially needed): Specify touches you actively crave for regulation or connection

Anna, a 30-year-old nurse, developed her touch map with her husband: "I realized I have very specific touch needs that change throughout the day. Morning hugs need to be firm and brief because I'm still waking up my nervous system. Evening cuddles can be longer and lighter because I'm more regulated. During stressful periods, I need deep pressure like tight hugs or back rubs. During calm periods, I can enjoy gentle touches like hand-holding or hair stroking. Mapping this out helped my husband understand that my changing responses weren't about him—they were about my nervous system."

Alternative intimacies: Creative ways to connect physically

Physical intimacy extends far beyond traditional sexual activity. AuDHD individuals often find alternative forms of physical connection that feel more comfortable and meaningful than conventional intimate activities.

These alternatives aren't "lesser than" traditional intimacy—they're different pathways to physical and emotional connection that work better for your unique nervous system.

Alternative intimate activities for AuDHD couples:

Parallel physical presence: Being physically close while engaged in separate, comfortable activities **Sensory sharing:** Exploring pleasant sensory experiences together like textured objects or calming scents **Movement-based connection:** Dancing, walking, or exercising together for physical bonding **Pressure-based intimacy:** Using weighted blankets, massage, or compression for calming connection **Temperature play:** Warm baths, ice cubes, or temperature contrasts for sensory exploration **Rhythmic activities:** Swinging, rocking, or other repetitive movements that regulate both partners

Creating intimacy through special interests: Many AuDHD individuals find that sharing special interests creates deeper intimacy than traditional romantic activities. Building models together, researching topics of mutual interest, or teaching each other new skills can create profound connection.

Sensory-friendly intimate alternatives:

For visual sensitivities: Intimacy in darkened rooms, with specific lighting, or with eyes closed **For auditory sensitivities:** Using noise-canceling headphones, white noise, or complete silence **For tactile sensitivities:** Experimenting with different fabrics, temperatures, or pressures **For vestibular sensitivities:** Avoiding position changes or movements that trigger dizziness **For proprioceptive needs:** Using firm touch, joint compression, or resistance activities

Consider Jake's experience as a 32-year-old librarian: "Traditional romantic activities like candlelit dinners or massage felt overwhelming to both me and my boyfriend. We discovered that we connect best through what we call 'research dates'—choosing a topic we're both curious about and spending the evening learning about it together. We'll read articles, watch documentaries, and discuss what we're learning. It might not sound romantic, but sharing intellectual curiosity and discovery feels incredibly intimate to us."

The gradual approach: Building tolerance vs. forcing through

One of the biggest mistakes in AuDHD relationships is trying to force tolerance for overwhelming sensory experiences. "Gradual exposure" doesn't mean enduring discomfort until you get used to it—it means slowly building positive associations with touch and physical intimacy at your nervous system's pace.

The difference between building tolerance and forcing through is crucial. Building tolerance involves slowly expanding your comfort zone with support and positive experiences. Forcing through involves enduring overwhelming sensations, which often leads to increased sensitivity and avoidance.

Principles for gradual sensory expansion:

Start with calm nervous system: Approach new sensory experiences when you're already regulated **Use positive associations:** Pair new sensations with things you already enjoy **Maintain control:** Always have the option to stop or modify the experience **Go at your pace:** Never rush based on external expectations or pressure **Celebrate small wins:** Acknowledge progress even if it seems minor to others **Respect limits:** Some sensitivities may never change, and that's okay

Practical gradual approach strategies:

For light touch sensitivity: Start with self-administered light touch when calm, then progress to partner-administered touch with your guidance

For position changes: Practice slow transitions between positions while maintaining physical contact and communication

For sensory environments: Gradually introduce new environmental factors one at a time rather than changing everything simultaneously

For duration tolerance: Start with brief positive experiences and slowly extend timing based on your comfort

Maria, a 29-year-old social worker, describes her gradual approach: "I used to think I hated all physical intimacy because light touch felt overwhelming. My partner and I started with just holding hands while watching movies. Then we progressed to brief hugs, then longer embraces with firm pressure. After months of positive experiences, I could even enjoy some light touch because my nervous system learned to associate physical contact with safety instead of overwhelm. The key was never pushing past my limits—we stopped whenever I felt uncomfortable."

Partner collaboration: Co-creating sensory solutions

Creating sensory-friendly intimacy requires active collaboration between partners. Your partner can't read your mind about sensory needs, and you can't anticipate all situations that might trigger sensory overwhelm. Ongoing communication and experimentation help you develop solutions together.

Framework for sensory collaboration:

Regular check-ins: Schedule specific times to discuss what's working and what isn't in your physical relationship **Experiment mindset:** Approach new activities as experiments rather than tests of your relationship **No-blame problem-solving:** Address sensory challenges as puzzles to solve together rather than relationship problems **Flexibility practice:** Both partners practice adapting when sensory needs change **Education sharing:** Learn about sensory processing together through books, articles, or workshops

Collaborative problem-solving process:

1. **Identify the challenge:** Specifically describe what sensory experience is problematic
2. **Brainstorm solutions:** Generate multiple possible modifications or alternatives
3. **Test options:** Try different approaches with low pressure and high communication
4. **Evaluate results:** Discuss what worked, what didn't, and why
5. **Refine approach:** Adjust based on what you learned and try again
6. **Document success:** Keep notes about what works for future reference

Quick Sensory Fixes for Common Issues

Issue: Room too bright for comfort **Fix:** Use adjustable lamps, blackout curtains, or eye masks

Issue: Background noise disruption **Fix:** White noise machines, earplugs for one partner, or soundproofing

Issue: Temperature differences between partners **Fix:** Separate blankets, fans, or heating pads for individual comfort

Issue: Touch sensitivity interfering with closeness **Fix:** Experiment with different pressures, fabrics, or timing

Issue: Overwhelm during intimate moments **Fix:** Develop hand signals for pause, continue, or stop

Practical Sensory Tools

Sensory Intimacy Mapping Worksheet

Create detailed maps for each sensory system:

Tactile preferences:

- Light touch responses: pleasant, neutral, or overwhelming
- Deep pressure needs: calming, neutral, or too much
- Temperature preferences: warm, cool, or room temperature
- Texture favorites: smooth, textured, soft, or firm

Environmental needs:

- Lighting: bright, dim, colored, or natural
- Sound: silence, white noise, music, or conversation
- Temperature: warm, cool, or variable
- Space: open, cozy, organized, or minimal

Timing considerations:

- Best times of day for physical intimacy
- Energy level requirements for different activities
- Sensory capacity changes throughout menstrual cycles, seasons, or stress levels
- Recovery time needed after sensory-intensive experiences

Environmental Modification Checklist

Lighting modifications:

- Install dimmer switches for adjustable lighting
- Use colored bulbs or filters for different moods
- Position lamps to avoid direct eye contact with light sources
- Consider blackout curtains for complete darkness options

Sound modifications:

- Add soft furnishings to reduce echo and harsh sounds
- Use white noise machines or apps to mask unpredictable sounds
- Position electronics away from intimate spaces to reduce buzzing
- Consider soundproofing for privacy and noise reduction

Temperature and air quality:

- Use fans or air conditioning for temperature control
- Consider separate bedding for different temperature needs
- Ensure good air circulation to prevent stuffiness
- Use air purifiers if scent sensitivity is an issue

Texture and comfort:

- Choose bedding materials based on sensory preferences
- Remove tags from clothing and fabrics
- Use weighted blankets for deep pressure needs
- Keep sensory comfort items nearby for regulation

Yes/No/Maybe Lists for Physical Connection

Create detailed lists to communicate boundaries clearly:

Yes list (always welcome):

- Specific types of touch you consistently enjoy
- Environmental conditions that always feel good
- Timing that works well for your nervous system
- Activities that consistently create positive connection

No list (not comfortable):

- Types of touch that feel overwhelming or irritating
- Environmental conditions that typically cause problems
- Timing that doesn't work due to sensory capacity
- Activities that consistently create overwhelm

Maybe list (depends on circumstances):

- Touch that feels good sometimes but not others
- Environmental factors that vary based on your current state
- Timing that works when you're regulated but not when stressed
- Activities you want to explore gradually or under specific conditions

Creating Your Sensory Love Story

Sensory intimacy in AuDHD relationships requires creativity, patience, and willingness to challenge conventional ideas about what physical connection should look like. Your nervous system's unique needs aren't obstacles to overcome—they're information to work with in creating intimate experiences that actually feel good for both partners.

The goal isn't to tolerate overwhelming sensory experiences or force yourself into neurotypical intimacy scripts. The goal is to discover forms of physical connection that honor your sensory needs while building genuine closeness with your partner.

This foundation of sensory understanding becomes crucial as you address other practical aspects of relationship management, including the executive function challenges that affect daily life together. Understanding how to create comfortable physical environments and respectful touch experiences provides the safety and regulation needed to tackle more complex relationship tasks.

Core Sensory Connection Principles

- Sensory needs in intimacy are neurological requirements, not preferences or pickiness
- Environmental modifications can transform overwhelming spaces into connecting ones
- Touch preferences vary across different types, pressures, and timing considerations
- Alternative forms of intimacy can be more connecting than traditional romantic scripts
- Gradual sensory expansion builds positive associations rather than forced tolerance

Chapter 7: Executive function hacks for two

The kitchen sink overflows with dishes while bills pile up on the counter. You both meant to handle these tasks, but somehow they never happened. Your ADHD brain keeps forgetting about the dishes until you desperately need a clean cup. Your autism brain wants a systematic approach to household management but can't figure out where to start. Meanwhile, your partner feels overwhelmed by the constant need to manage these daily life details.

This scenario repeats across countless AuDHD relationships. Executive function challenges—difficulty with planning, organization, time management, and task completion—affect how you navigate daily life together. But these aren't character flaws or signs of laziness. They're neurological differences that require specific strategies and systems.

Research from Embrace Autism and Psychology Today confirms that executive function challenges are central to both autism and ADHD experiences. Having both conditions often means facing these challenges from multiple angles simultaneously, requiring creative solutions that work with your unique brain rather than against it.

The executive function tango: When both partners struggle

Executive function includes several key cognitive skills: working memory, cognitive flexibility, planning and prioritization, task initiation, organization, time management, and impulse control. Different people struggle with different aspects, and AuDHD individuals often face challenges across multiple areas.

The complexity multiplies when both partners have executive function differences. You might both struggle with remembering to pay bills, or both have difficulty initiating household tasks. Traditional relationship advice assumes that one partner can compensate for the other's weaknesses, but that doesn't work when you both face similar challenges.

Consider Lisa and Mark, both diagnosed with AuDHD, describing their household management struggles: "We both have great intentions about keeping the house organized, but we both struggle with task initiation. We'll look at the messy living room and both think 'someone should clean this up,' but neither of us can figure out how to start. We end up in these weird standoffs where we both know something needs to happen but we're both stuck."

Their experience illustrates how dual executive function challenges require different approaches than typical relationship dynamics. Instead of one partner compensating for the other, both partners need external systems and structures to support their shared challenges.

Common executive function challenge combinations:

Both partners struggle with time management: Constantly running late, underestimating task duration, losing track of time **Both have working memory issues:** Forgetting appointments, losing important items, not following through on commitments **Both struggle with task initiation:** Knowing what needs to be done but being unable to start **Both have organization challenges:** Difficulty maintaining systems, losing track of belongings, struggling with paperwork **Both face planning difficulties:** Trouble breaking large tasks into steps, difficulty anticipating needs, poor long-term planning

Task initiation vs. completion: Bridging the gap together

One of the most common executive function splits in AuDHD relationships involves task initiation versus task completion challenges. One partner might be great at starting projects but terrible at finishing them. The other might excel at completing tasks once started but struggle with taking the first step.

Understanding these different challenge patterns helps you leverage each other's strengths rather than becoming frustrated by apparent inconsistencies.

Task initiation challenges:

- Difficulty taking the first step on projects
- Procrastination despite good intentions
- Feeling overwhelmed by large or undefined tasks
- Needing external prompts or accountability to start
- Perfectionism that prevents beginning imperfect efforts

Task completion challenges:

- Starting multiple projects but finishing few
- Getting distracted before reaching endpoints
- Losing motivation as novelty wears off
- Difficulty with detail work required for completion
- Moving on to new interesting tasks before finishing current ones

Bridging strategies for different challenge types:

If one partner initiates well and the other completes well: Use the initiator to start projects and the completer to finish them, with clear handoff points and communication about progress.

If both struggle with initiation: Create external accountability systems, use body doubling (working alongside each other), and break tasks into smaller, more manageable first steps.

If both struggle with completion: Build celebration and reward systems for finishing projects, use time limits to create urgency, and focus on "good enough" standards rather than perfection.

Take Sarah's experience as a 31-year-old graphic designer: "My husband is amazing at research and planning—he can spend hours organizing the perfect approach to organizing our garage. But he never actually starts the physical work. I'm terrible at planning but once someone tells me 'start here,' I can work for hours. We learned to use his planning brain to create step-by-step lists, then I follow the lists while he handles the thinking parts. It's like having one complete executive function brain between us."

Memory systems that actually work: External brain strategies

AuDHD individuals often struggle with working memory—holding information in mind while using it for complex tasks. This affects everything from following multi-step directions to remembering conversations that happened yesterday. Creating external memory systems becomes essential for relationship functioning.

Types of memory challenges affecting relationships:

Working memory: Difficulty holding multiple pieces of information in mind simultaneously **Prospective memory:** Forgetting to do things you intend to do in the future **Episodic memory:** Difficulty remembering specific events or conversations accurately **Sequential memory:** Trouble remembering the order of steps or events **Associative memory:** Problems connecting related information across different contexts

External memory systems for couples:

Shared digital calendars with automatic reminders for both personal and couple commitments **Task management apps** that allow both partners to see and update household responsibilities **Voice recording systems** for capturing important conversations or decisions **Physical reminder systems** like bulletin boards, sticky notes, or designated spots for important items **Photo documentation** of important events, decisions, or household organization systems

The relationship memory bank concept:

Create a shared system for documenting important relationship information:

- **Conversation summaries** for major decisions or agreements
- **Event documentation** with photos and notes from special occasions
- **Preference tracking** for gifts, date ideas, and individual needs
- **Problem-solving records** documenting what worked for recurring challenges
- **Growth documentation** tracking relationship progress and positive changes

Michael, a 33-year-old teacher, explains his couple's memory system: "We use a shared note-taking app where we document everything from date night ideas to arguments we've resolved. It sounds unromantic, but it's actually brought us closer because we can remember positive things about each other instead of only focusing on current problems. Plus, we never have the same argument twice because we can look up what we decided last time."

The getting-stuck phenomenon: Mutual support protocols

"Getting stuck" is a common executive function experience where you know what you need to do but can't make yourself do it. It's not laziness or lack of motivation—it's a neurological barrier that prevents task initiation or continuation. The experience feels like being behind an invisible wall that prevents action despite clear intention.

Having mutual support protocols for stuck episodes prevents the shame and frustration that often accompanies these experiences. Instead of blaming each other for not doing obvious tasks, you can recognize stuckness as a neurological event that requires specific intervention strategies.

Signs of executive function stuckness:

Physical manifestations: Feeling frozen, restless energy with no direction, physical tension or fatigue **Cognitive signs:** Knowing what to do but being unable to start, circular thinking without action, feeling overwhelmed by simple tasks **Emotional indicators:** Frustration, shame, anxiety about not doing obvious things, feeling lazy despite caring deeply **Behavioral patterns:** Procrastination, task switching without completion, avoiding the stuck area entirely

Mutual unsticking strategies:

Body doubling: Working alongside each other for motivation and accountability **Task breaking:** Helping each other divide overwhelming tasks into smaller, manageable steps **Environmental changes:** Moving to different locations or modifying current space to reset mental state **Accountability partnerships:** Gentle check-ins and progress sharing without judgment **Parallel processing:** Working on separate tasks simultaneously for mutual motivation

Emergency unsticking protocols:

When one partner is stuck:

1. **Recognize without judgment:** "It looks like you might be stuck. What's happening?"
2. **Offer specific support:** "Would body doubling help, or do you need me to break this down into steps?"
3. **Provide external motivation:** "I'll set a timer for 15 minutes and we'll both work on our stuck tasks."
4. **Celebrate small action:** "Great job taking that first step. What feels like the next small thing?"

When both partners are stuck simultaneously:

1. **Acknowledge the situation:** "We're both stuck. This is a neurological thing, not a character flaw."
2. **Change the environment:** Leave the house, switch rooms, or modify the current space somehow.
3. **Use external accountability:** Call a friend, set public commitments, or use apps with social features.
4. **Focus on smallest possible action:** Commit to doing just one tiny step without pressure for more.

Time blindness solutions: Making peace with scheduling

Time blindness—difficulty accurately perceiving the passage of time—creates ongoing challenges for AuDHD individuals and their relationships. You might consistently underestimate how long tasks will take, lose track of time during enjoyable activities, or struggle with concepts like "running late."

The key to managing time blindness isn't learning to perceive time better—it's developing external systems that compensate for your brain's different relationship with temporal awareness.

How time blindness affects relationships:

Scheduling conflicts from underestimating task duration or transition time **Chronic lateness** causing stress and conflict with time-conscious partners **Hyperfocus time loss** where special interests cause you to miss appointments or commitments **Poor boundary estimation** leading to overcommitment and relationship strain **Different time perspectives** where "soon" means different things to different partners

External time management systems:

Multiple alarm systems with specific purposes and different sounds for different types of reminders **Time estimation practice** by documenting actual task duration versus estimates **Buffer time scheduling** by adding extra time between activities and appointments **Visual time tools** like analog clocks, timers, or time-tracking apps that show time passage **Accountability partnerships** where partners help with time awareness and gentle reminders

The "Good Enough" time management approach:

Perfect time management isn't the goal—functional time management is. Focus on systems that reduce conflict and stress rather than achieving neurotypical time precision.

- **Aim for "close enough" rather than exact timing**
- **Build flexibility into schedules rather than rigid time adherence**

- **Communicate estimated arrival times rather than promising exact times**
- **Focus on reducing lateness impact rather than eliminating all lateness**
- **Celebrate improvements rather than demanding perfection**

Jenny, a 30-year-old nurse, developed her time blindness accommodation system: "I stopped trying to be on time and started trying to be less late. I set alarms for everything—getting in the shower, leaving the house, even switching between tasks. My husband learned that 'I'll be ready in 10 minutes' actually means 20-25 minutes, so he plans accordingly. It's not perfect, but it's way less stressful than constantly fighting about time."

Preventing the shame spiral: Compassionate accountability

Executive function challenges often trigger shame cycles that damage relationships more than the original challenges themselves. When you struggle with basic tasks like paying bills or cleaning house, it's easy to feel like you're failing as a partner. This shame can lead to hiding struggles, avoiding conversations, or becoming defensive about feedback.

Compassionate accountability separates the person from the challenge while still addressing relationship impact. It acknowledges that executive function struggles are neurological rather than character-based while maintaining expectations for finding workable solutions.

Elements of compassionate accountability:

Separate person from problem: "You're not lazy or irresponsible. Your brain works differently, and we need systems that support how it actually functions."

Focus on impact rather than intent: "I know you didn't mean to forget our anniversary. The impact was that I felt unimportant. How can we prevent this from happening again?"

Collaborate on solutions: "This isn't working for either of us. Let's brainstorm different approaches that might work better."

Acknowledge effort over outcome: "I can see you're working hard on this. What's making it difficult, and how can I support you?"

Address shame directly: "You seem to be feeling bad about yourself. These challenges are neurological, not character flaws."

Shame spiral intervention strategies:

For the struggling partner:

- Practice self-compassion language: "I'm doing my best with a challenging brain"
- Share struggles early rather than hiding them until they become crises
- Ask for specific support rather than general understanding
- Separate worth from productivity or task completion

For the supporting partner:

- Respond to struggles with curiosity rather than frustration
- Offer practical support rather than emotional reassurance alone
- Maintain your own boundaries while supporting your partner's challenges
- Address relationship impact without attacking your partner's character

Practical Executive Function Tools

Relationship Management System Setup Guide

Create a shared system for managing household and relationship responsibilities:

Step 1: Inventory current challenges List all areas where executive function issues create relationship stress or conflict.

Step 2: Identify strength patterns Determine which partner is stronger in which executive function areas, if any patterns exist.

Step 3: Choose management tools Select apps, systems, or tools that both partners can access and update easily.

Step 4: Assign responsibility types Decide who manages which types of tasks based on strength patterns and preferences.

Step 5: Create backup systems Develop protocols for when primary systems fail or when both partners are struggling.

Step 6: Schedule regular reviews Plan monthly check-ins to assess what's working and what needs adjustment.

Executive Function Strengths/Challenges Mapper

Each partner completes this assessment:

Planning and organization:

- Strength level (1-10) in creating step-by-step plans
- Strength level in maintaining organizational systems
- Specific challenges in planning or organization
- Successful strategies you've used in these areas

Time management:

- Strength level in accurately estimating task duration
- Strength level in arriving on time to commitments
- Specific challenges with time awareness or scheduling
- Tools or strategies that help with time management

Task completion:

- Strength level in initiating new tasks or projects
- Strength level in following through to completion
- Specific challenges in starting or finishing tasks
- Environmental factors that support task completion

Memory and attention:

- Strength level in remembering appointments and commitments
- Strength level in maintaining focus during tasks
- Specific challenges with memory or attention
- External supports that help with memory and focus

Household Task-Sharing Algorithm

Create fair distribution based on executive function strengths:

High-initiation tasks (easy to start, may need completion support):

- Quick cleaning tasks
- Simple meal preparation
- Routine maintenance activities

High-completion tasks (need help starting but can finish independently):

- Detailed projects
- Research-based activities
- Systematic organization

High-structure tasks (need clear systems and external reminders):

- Bill paying
- Appointment scheduling
- Paperwork management

High-flexibility tasks (can be done on variable schedules):

- Household maintenance
- Shopping
- Meal planning

Emergency Unsticking Strategies

Quick reset techniques:

- Change physical location or body position
- Set a 10-minute timer for any small action
- Use the "next smallest step" approach
- Get physical movement or sensory input

Partner support strategies:

- Offer to work alongside without taking over the task
- Help break down the stuck task into smaller pieces
- Provide external accountability through check-ins
- Suggest environmental changes that might help

System-level strategies:

- Review whether the stuck task needs to be done at all
- Consider alternative approaches or methods
- Delegate to someone else if possible
- Schedule the task for a different time when energy might be higher

Building Your Executive Function Partnership

Executive function challenges don't have to derail your relationship. With understanding, appropriate systems, and mutual support, you can build approaches that work with your combined neurological realities rather than against them.

The goal isn't to eliminate all executive function struggles—it's to develop sustainable systems that reduce relationship conflict while honoring both partners' neurological differences. This requires ongoing experimentation, regular system adjustments, and lots of self-compassion for both partners.

These executive function management skills become the foundation for the next crucial relationship element: creating clear communication about your needs, preferences, and operating instructions. A relationship user manual helps partners understand each other's unique requirements and preferences, building on the practical systems you've developed for daily life management.

Core Executive Function Partnership Strategies

- Executive function challenges are neurological differences requiring external systems, not character flaws
- Different challenge patterns between partners can become complementary strengths with proper coordination
- External memory systems compensate for working memory difficulties affecting relationship management
- Getting stuck is a common neurological experience requiring specific intervention protocols rather than criticism
- Compassionate accountability addresses relationship impact while maintaining understanding of neurological differences

Chapter 8: Creating your relationship user manual

Your partner loves you, but they have no idea that asking "How was your day?" while you're still processing the transition from work to home feels overwhelming. They don't know that you need fifteen minutes of quiet time before you can engage in conversation, or that unexpected phone calls trigger your anxiety, or that you communicate love through sharing articles about your special interests.

Meanwhile, you love your partner but you're constantly guessing about their needs. Do they want advice or just listening when they share problems? How do they prefer to receive feedback? What does emotional support look like for them? You're both navigating your relationship without clear instructions for how to support each other effectively.

This is why you need relationship user manuals—detailed guides that explain how you each operate, what you need, and how partners can support you most effectively. These aren't rigid rules or demands; they're communication tools that make the implicit explicit.

Why you need a user manual: Making the implicit explicit

Most relationship advice assumes that people will naturally learn each other's needs through time and observation. But AuDHD brains often struggle with implicit social information. You might miss subtle cues about your partner's emotional state or communication preferences. They might misinterpret your behaviors because they don't understand the neurological basis for your responses.

User manuals translate neurological differences into clear, actionable information. Instead of your partner guessing why you seem withdrawn after social events, your manual explains that you need recovery time and aren't rejecting them. Instead of you wondering why your partner seems frustrated with your long explanations, their manual clarifies that they prefer brief, direct communication.

The process of creating user manuals also increases self-awareness. Many AuDHD individuals have spent so much time masking or adapting to others' expectations that they've lost touch with their own genuine needs and preferences. Writing your manual helps you identify and articulate your authentic operating requirements.

Consider Rachel's experience as a 29-year-old therapist: "I used to think I was high-maintenance because I had so many specific needs around communication timing, sensory environments, and emotional processing. Creating my user manual helped me realize these weren't unreasonable demands—they were legitimate accommodations for how my brain works. When my girlfriend read my manual, she said 'Oh, this makes so much sense. I thought you were upset with me when you needed space, but you were just regulating your nervous system.'"

Rachel's experience demonstrates how user manuals prevent misinterpretation of neurological needs as relationship problems.

Benefits of relationship user manuals:

Reduce guesswork about how to support each other during difficult times **Prevent misunderstandings** caused by different communication styles or processing needs
Increase intimacy through detailed knowledge of each other's inner experiences **Provide reference** during conflicts or confusing relationship moments **Support advocacy** by giving partners language to explain your needs to others **Document growth** as you learn more about yourselves and update your manuals

The components: What to include in your guide

Effective user manuals cover all aspects of how you function in relationships—from daily logistics to emotional needs to crisis management. The goal is creating a document that helps your partner understand and support you across different situations and emotional states.

Essential sections for AuDHD relationship user manuals:

Basic operating information:

- Optimal communication timing and methods
- Sensory accommodations needed in shared spaces
- Energy management and recovery requirements
- Processing time needs for decisions and emotional topics

Communication preferences:

- How you express different emotions and what they mean
- Preferred methods for receiving feedback or criticism
- What different types of silence or withdrawal indicate
- How to approach you when you seem upset or overwhelmed

Support protocols:

- What helps when you're dysregulated, shutdown, or melting down
- How to provide comfort during difficult emotional states
- When to offer advice versus when to just listen
- Physical comfort preferences and boundaries

Relationship maintenance:

- How you express and prefer to receive love and appreciation
- Conflict resolution approaches that work for your brain
- How to handle disagreements without triggering shame or shutdown
- Recovery protocols after arguments or misunderstandings

Crisis management:

- Warning signs that you're approaching overload or burnout

- Immediate intervention strategies for emotional or sensory overwhelm
- When and how to seek additional support or professional help
- How to communicate needs when verbal communication becomes difficult

Daily life logistics:

- Household management preferences and challenges
- Social energy limitations and recovery requirements
- Schedule flexibility versus structure needs
- Financial management approaches and triggers

Take Michael's comprehensive manual as a 34-year-old programmer: "My user manual has sections for everything from 'How to know if I'm having a shutdown' to 'Why I need to research everything before making decisions.' The most helpful part for my husband was the emotional regulation section that explains why I sometimes need to leave the room during conversations—it's not rejection, it's regulation. Having this written down means he doesn't take my coping strategies personally."

Translating needs into requests: Specific vs. vague communication

One of the biggest challenges in relationships is translating internal experiences into specific, actionable requests. Many people know what they need but struggle to communicate those needs in ways their partner can understand and implement.

AuDHD individuals often have very specific needs that seem obvious to them but aren't intuitive to others. Learning to translate these needs into clear requests prevents frustration and improves the likelihood of getting appropriate support.

Common translation challenges:

Internal experience: "I'm overwhelmed" **Vague request:** "I need space" **Specific request:** "I need 30 minutes alone in our bedroom with no interruptions to regulate my nervous system"

Internal experience: "This conversation is too much" **Vague request:** "Can we talk about this later?" **Specific request:** "I'm hitting my processing limit. Can we pause this conversation and schedule time tomorrow evening to continue?"

Internal experience: "I can't handle social demands right now" **Vague request:** "I don't want to go out" **Specific request:** "I'm at my social energy limit for today. Can we either stay home or go somewhere quiet where we don't have to interact with other people?"

The CLEAR request framework:

Concrete: Specify exactly what action you need **Logical:** Explain the reasoning behind your request **Emotional:** Share how you're feeling and what you're experiencing **Actionable:** Make it something your partner can actually do **Reasonable:** Ensure the request is fair and possible to fulfill

Needs-to-requests translation examples:

Need: Recovery time after social events **Translation:** "After social events, I need 1-2 hours of quiet time to process and recharge. This means no conversation, questions, or requests during that time. It's not about you—it's how my nervous system recovers from social stimulation."

Need: Processing time for emotional conversations **Translation:** "When we discuss emotional topics, I need time to think before responding. If you ask me how I feel about something, I need at least 10 minutes to identify and organize my thoughts. Can you ask the question and then we both do something else while I process?"

Need: Sensory accommodations during intimacy **Translation:** "For physical intimacy, I need the room to be slightly cool, with soft lighting and no background noise. Sudden sounds or bright lights can trigger sensory overwhelm that shuts down my ability to be present with you."

Your partner's manual: Encouraging mutual documentation

User manuals work best when both partners create them. Having only one manual creates an imbalance where one person's needs are explicitly documented while the other's remain implicit. Mutual documentation ensures both partners' needs are equally understood and respected.

Some partners initially resist creating their own manuals, especially if they don't identify as neurodivergent. They might say "I don't have special needs" or "I'm pretty easy-going." But everyone has preferences, triggers, and optimal support strategies—neurotypical people just aren't usually asked to document them explicitly.

Encouraging mutual manual creation:

Frame it as relationship enhancement: "This will help us both support each other better" rather than "You need to accommodate my differences"

Start with easy sections: Begin with preferences like communication timing or conflict resolution rather than complex emotional needs

Use examples from their experience: "Remember how you prefer to process work stress before talking about household stuff? That would be great to include in your manual."

Emphasize mutual benefit: "I want to support you as well as you support me. Knowing your preferences helps me be a better partner."

Make it collaborative: Work on your manuals together, sharing sections and asking questions about each other's entries

Normalize the process: "Lots of couples do this. It's like having an instruction manual for how to love each other well."

Sample prompts for partner manual creation:

Communication preferences: How do you like to receive feedback? What's the best way to approach you when you're stressed?

Emotional support: When you're upset, do you want advice or just listening? How do you prefer physical comfort?

Conflict resolution: What helps you stay calm during disagreements? How do you prefer to resolve arguments?

Daily life: What's your ideal morning routine? How do you prefer to handle household decisions?

Stress management: What are your warning signs for overwhelm? What helps you relax and recharge?

Using your manuals: From theory to daily practice

Creating user manuals is only the first step—using them effectively requires integration into daily relationship practices. The manuals should become living documents that you reference regularly, not one-time exercises that gather digital dust.

Daily manual integration strategies:

Reference during conflicts: "Let me check your manual to see how you prefer to handle disagreements" **Proactive support:** "Your manual says you need downtime after work. I'll give you space until dinner" **Clarification tool:** "I'm not sure if you need advice or listening right now. What does your manual say about this situation?" **Advocacy resource:** "My manual explains why I need these accommodations. Can we review it together?" **Growth tracking:** "I've learned something new about my needs. I want to update my manual."

Weekly manual review practices:

Schedule regular times to discuss how well you're both following the manual guidance and what adjustments might be needed. This prevents the manuals from becoming outdated or ignored.

Monthly manual updates:

Relationships and self-awareness evolve. Set aside time monthly to review and update your manuals based on new learning about yourselves and each other.

Crisis manual consultation:

During relationship difficulties, return to the manuals for guidance rather than making assumptions about each other's needs or motivations.

Lisa, a 32-year-old social worker, explains her manual usage: "We keep our manuals bookmarked on our phones and reference them constantly. When my boyfriend seems stressed, I check his manual for his preferred support strategies instead of guessing. When I'm overwhelmed, he looks up my regulation techniques instead of trying random things that might not help. It takes the guesswork out of supporting each other."

Updates and evolution: Keeping manuals current

Self-awareness and relationship needs change over time. Your manual should evolve as you learn more about yourself, as your life circumstances change, and as your relationship develops deeper levels of intimacy and understanding.

Common reasons for manual updates:

Increased self-awareness from therapy, personal growth, or new experiences **Life changes** like job stress, health issues, or major transitions

Relationship development as you become more comfortable sharing vulnerabilities **External stressors** that temporarily or permanently change your needs **Successful experimentation** with new support strategies or accommodation approaches **Failed strategies** that need to be removed or modified in your manual

Manual versioning system:

Keep dated versions of your manuals so you can track how your needs and self-understanding have changed over time. This can be valuable information for both you and your partner.

Collaborative updating process:

Review manuals together regularly and ask each other questions like:

- "What's working well from your manual?"
- "What seems outdated or needs modification?"
- "What have we learned about you that should be added?"
- "Are there new situations or stressors we should address?"

User Manual Quick Start Examples

Communication section sample: "I process information slowly and need time to formulate responses to emotional questions. If you ask how I feel about something, I need at least 10 minutes to think before I can give you a meaningful answer. Saying 'I don't know' doesn't mean I don't care—it means I need more processing time."

Support section sample: "When I'm overwhelmed, I shut down and can't talk. This looks like staring at nothing or leaving the room suddenly. What helps: dim lighting, no questions or conversation, and physical space. What doesn't help: asking if I'm okay repeatedly or trying to fix the situation immediately."

Conflict section sample: "During arguments, I get flooded with emotions and can't think clearly. I need to pause conflicts and return to them later when I'm regulated. This isn't avoidance—it's ensuring I can communicate effectively instead of saying things I'll regret."

Practical Manual Creation Tools

Relationship User Manual Template

Section 1: Basic Information

- Preferred communication methods and timing
- Energy patterns throughout the day/week/month
- Sensory accommodations needed in shared spaces
- Processing time requirements for decisions

Section 2: Emotional Support

- How I express different emotions and what they mean
- What I need when I'm upset, stressed, or overwhelmed
- How I prefer to receive comfort and reassurance
- Warning signs that I'm approaching my limits

Section 3: Communication

- How I best receive feedback or constructive criticism
- What different types of silence or withdrawal mean
- How to approach me when I seem upset or distant
- My conflict resolution style and preferences

Section 4: Daily Life

- Household management strengths and challenges
- Social energy limitations and recovery needs
- Schedule preferences and flexibility requirements
- Financial decision-making style and triggers

Section 5: Crisis Management

- Signs that I'm heading toward shutdown, meltdown, or burnout
- Immediate strategies that help during overwhelming moments

- When and how to suggest additional support or professional help
- How to support me when verbal communication becomes difficult

Manual Sharing Conversation Guide

Opening the conversation: "I've created a user manual to help you understand how I work best in our relationship. It's not a list of demands—it's information to help you support me effectively while I learn to support you better too."

Explaining the purpose: "This covers everything from how I communicate emotions to what helps when I'm overwhelmed. Think of it as instructions for how to love me in ways that actually feel good to my nervous system."

Encouraging questions: "Please ask questions about anything that seems unclear or doesn't make sense. I want this to be a helpful tool, not confusing documentation."

Requesting reciprocity: "I'd love to help you create your own manual so I can support you better too. Everyone has preferences and optimal support strategies—yours just might not be written down yet."

Setting update expectations: "This is a living document that I'll update as I learn more about myself. I'll let you know when I make changes, and I hope you'll tell me when something isn't working or needs clarification."

Building Your Relationship Navigation System

User manuals transform relationships from guessing games into collaborative partnerships based on clear understanding and mutual support. They provide roadmaps for navigating each other's inner worlds while honoring neurological differences that might otherwise create conflict or misunderstanding.

The process of creating and using these manuals builds intimacy through detailed knowledge of each other's authentic needs and preferences. Instead of trying to be the partner you think they want, you can learn to be the partner they actually need.

This foundation of clear communication and documented understanding becomes crucial as you face the inevitable conflicts and challenges that arise in any long-term relationship. Having explicit information about each other's operating systems makes conflict resolution and emotional repair much more effective and less damaging to your connection.

Manual Mastery Fundamentals

- User manuals make implicit relationship needs explicit, reducing guesswork and misunderstanding
- Effective manuals translate internal experiences into specific, actionable requests for support
- Mutual documentation ensures both partners' needs are equally understood and respected
- Regular updates keep manuals current as self-awareness and relationship needs evolve
- Active manual usage in daily life transforms theoretical understanding into practical relationship enhancement

Chapter 9: The conflict resolution remix

The argument started over dirty dishes, but now you're screaming about everything wrong with your relationship while your partner sits in stunned silence. Your ADHD brain is firing rapid-fire accusations, your autism brain is cataloging every injustice from the past six months, and your nervous system is completely dysregulated. Meanwhile, your partner doesn't understand why asking you to help with dishes turned into World War Three.

This is conflict through the AuDHD lens—intense, overwhelming, and often completely disproportionate to the original trigger. Your neurological differences don't just affect how you communicate during calm moments; they fundamentally change how you experience and navigate relationship conflicts.

Traditional conflict resolution advice assumes everyone can stay rational during disagreements, take turns speaking, and work toward compromise. But your AuDHD brain doesn't function that way during conflict. You might shut down completely, become hyperverbal and interrupt constantly, or experience such intense emotions that logical thinking becomes impossible.

Understanding how your neurology affects conflict helps you develop personalized strategies that actually work with your brain rather than against it.

Conflict through the AuDHD lens: Why fights feel different

Research from Embrace Autism shows that neurodivergent individuals experience conflict differently than neurotypical people. Your autism contributes systematic thinking, intense emotional responses, and difficulty with ambiguous social situations. Your ADHD adds impulsivity, emotional dysregulation, and attention challenges during heated moments.

These neurological differences create conflict experiences that feel more intense, last longer, and are harder to resolve than typical relationship disagreements.

How autism affects conflict:

Literal interpretation can turn simple requests into perceived criticism **Intense emotional responses** make small disagreements feel catastrophic **Difficulty reading social cues** during conflict leads to misunderstanding partner's intentions **Systematic thinking** brings up related issues and past examples during current conflicts **Sensory overwhelm** from raised voices or emotional intensity can trigger shutdown

How ADHD affects conflict:

Emotional dysregulation creates intense reactions that feel overwhelming **Impulsivity** leads to saying things you regret before thinking them through **Attention difficulties** make it hard to follow complex emotional conversations **Working memory issues** affect your ability to track multiple points during discussions **Rejection sensitivity** interprets conflict as relationship-ending threats

The AuDHD conflict multiplier effect:

When autism and ADHD combine during conflict, you get simultaneous experiences that seem contradictory but are completely real:

- Wanting to process carefully AND needing to respond immediately
- Feeling overwhelmed by emotion AND needing logical resolution
- Craving detailed discussion AND being unable to focus on conversation
- Needing space AND fearing abandonment if you leave the conflict

Consider Maria's experience as a 30-year-old teacher: "During arguments with my boyfriend, I feel like I'm being pulled in opposite directions. My autism brain wants to discuss every detail and make sure we resolve everything properly. My ADHD brain is so emotionally flooded that I can't think straight and just want the conflict to stop. I end up either talking in circles for hours or completely shutting down and leaving the room. Neither approach actually resolves anything."

Maria's experience illustrates how AuDHD creates internal conflict during external conflict, making resolution more complex than simple communication techniques can address.

The STOP technique adapted: Pause protocols for heated moments

The Cincinnati Center for DBT developed the STOP technique for managing emotional overwhelm, but the standard version needs adaptation for AuDHD brains. Your neurology requires more specific protocols that account for both autism and ADHD needs during dysregulated moments.

Traditional STOP technique:

- **S**top what you're doing
- **T**ake a breath
- **O**bserve the situation
- **P**roceed with awareness

AuDHD-adapted STOP protocol:

Safety first - Remove yourself from sensory overwhelm and create physical safety **T**ime and space - Take extended processing time, not just a single breath **O**utside perspective - Use external tools to gain clarity about the situation **P**ause before returning - Plan your re-entry to the conversation carefully

Implementing the adapted STOP technique:

Safety first: Immediately address sensory overwhelm by dimming lights, reducing noise, or moving to a calmer environment. Your nervous system can't regulate while being bombarded with overwhelming input.

Time and space: Take significantly more time than neurotypical advice suggests. You might need 20 minutes or even several hours to process intense emotions and return to logical thinking.

Outside perspective: Use written tools like journaling, voice recordings to yourself, or texting a trusted friend to gain clarity about what's actually happening versus what your dysregulated brain is telling you.

Pause before returning: Plan how you'll re-enter the conversation, what you want to communicate, and what outcome you're seeking before returning to discuss the conflict.

Take David's implementation as a 32-year-old engineer: "I used to think taking a break during arguments was giving up or avoiding the problem. Now I tell my wife 'I need to implement my STOP protocol' and go to our spare room for at least 30 minutes. I write down what I'm feeling, what the actual issue is versus what my emotions are telling me, and what I want from the conversation. When I come back, I'm regulated enough to actually problem-solve instead of just reacting."

De-escalation in 30 Seconds

When conflict is escalating rapidly:

1. **Signal the need for pause:** "I'm getting dysregulated and need to pause"
2. **Set a specific return time:** "Let's come back to this in one hour"
3. **Leave the environment:** Physically move to a different space
4. **Use immediate regulation:** Cold water on face, deep breathing, or movement

Managing the meltdown-conflict intersection: Safety first strategies

Sometimes conflicts trigger meltdowns or shutdowns—neurological responses that make continued discussion impossible. These aren't manipulation tactics or emotional immaturity; they're legitimate neurological events that require specific management strategies.

Recognizing pre-meltdown signs during conflict:

- Increased stimming or repetitive movements
- Difficulty finding words or communicating clearly
- Sensory sensitivity increases (sounds seem louder, lights brighter)
- Physical symptoms like tight chest, rapid heartbeat, or nausea
- Feeling like you need to escape or hide

Shutdown warning signs during conflict:

- Sudden inability to speak or respond
- Feeling disconnected from your body or emotions
- Overwhelming fatigue or heaviness
- Difficulty processing what your partner is saying
- Urge to withdraw completely from the situation

Safety protocols for meltdown-conflict intersection:

Immediate safety: Both partners recognize that continuing the conflict during meltdown is unsafe and unproductive

Environmental modification: Reduce sensory input immediately—dim lights, lower voices, eliminate background noise

No pressure to continue: The dysregulated partner gets space without guilt or pressure to "finish the conversation"

Care without enabling: The supporting partner provides comfort without taking responsibility for solving the conflict

Return when regulated: Resume the discussion only when the dysregulated partner's nervous system has returned to baseline

Sample scripts for meltdown during conflict:

For the dysregulated partner: "I'm having a meltdown and can't continue this conversation safely right now. I need space to regulate and we'll return to this later."

For the supporting partner: "I can see you're overwhelmed. Let's pause this conversation. What do you need right now to feel safe?"

For resuming later: "I'm feeling more regulated now. Are you ready to return to our conversation from earlier, or do you need more time too?"

Consider Sarah's experience as a 28-year-old social worker: "I used to try to push through meltdowns during arguments because I thought taking a break meant I was 'losing' the fight. But continuing to argue during a meltdown just made everything worse. Now my husband and I have an agreement that if either of us says 'meltdown protocol,' we immediately stop the argument and focus on safety and regulation. We return to the issue later when I'm not in crisis mode."

Time-outs that work: Honoring processing differences

Traditional relationship advice suggests brief cool-down periods during conflicts, but AuDHD brains often need significantly more time to process emotions and return to productive discussion. Creating time-out protocols that honor your processing differences prevents conflicts from escalating while ensuring issues actually get resolved.

Why AuDHD time-outs need to be different:

Processing time variations: Your autism brain might need hours to organize thoughts and feelings **Emotional regulation differences:** Your ADHD brain might take longer to return to baseline after emotional flooding **Sensory recovery needs:** You might need time to recover from sensory overwhelm before continuing discussion **Executive function restoration:** Complex thinking skills need time to come back online after dysregulation

Effective time-out protocols for AuDHD:

Predetermined agreements: Establish time-out rules during calm moments, not during conflicts **Specific timeframes:** Set clear expectations for how long the break will last **Return responsibility:** The person requesting time-out is responsible for returning to the conversation **No punishment:** Time-outs aren't consequences; they're neurological accommodations **Progress acknowledgment:** Recognize that needing time-outs is self-awareness, not avoidance

Time-out implementation framework:

1. **Signal clearly:** "I need a time-out to process this effectively"
2. **Set specific timing:** "I'll be ready to continue this conversation tomorrow evening"
3. **Honor the timeframe:** Return at the agreed time even if you don't feel completely ready
4. **Use processing time effectively:** Journal, walk, or use other regulation strategies
5. **Re-enter thoughtfully:** Come back with specific thoughts about the issue, not just cooled emotions

Lisa, a 31-year-old nurse, developed her time-out system: "My girlfriend used to get frustrated when I needed breaks during arguments because she wanted to resolve things immediately. Now we have an agreement that I can call time-outs for up to 24 hours, but I have to return at the time I specify. I use that time to figure out what I'm actually upset about versus what my emotions are telling me. When I come back, I can communicate clearly instead of just reacting."

The repair ritual: Reconnecting after conflict

AuDHD individuals often struggle with the emotional aftermath of conflicts. Your autism brain might continue processing the argument for days, analyzing what was said and what it meant. Your ADHD brain might feel overwhelmed by the intensity and want to avoid similar conversations in the future.

Creating specific repair rituals helps you reconnect after conflicts while honoring your neurological needs for processing and reassurance.

Components of AuDHD repair rituals:

Acknowledgment of impact: Both partners acknowledge how the conflict affected them without blame **Specific apologies:** Clear statements about what each person will do differently **Reassurance about the relationship:** Explicit statements that the conflict doesn't threaten your connection **Plan for prevention:** Concrete strategies to handle similar situations differently in the future **Physical or emotional reconnection:** Appropriate gestures that rebuild intimacy

Sample repair ritual process:

Step 1: Check readiness "Are you ready to talk about our argument from yesterday, or do you need more processing time?"

Step 2: Share impact "Here's how that conflict affected me..." (without blame or criticism)

Step 3: Take responsibility "I take responsibility for..." (specific behaviors, not general character flaws)

Step 4: Request changes "What I need going forward is..." (specific, actionable requests)

Step 5: Reconnect Physical affection, shared activity, or verbal affirmations that rebuild connection

Step 6: Plan prevention "Next time this issue comes up, we'll..." (concrete strategies)

Take Michael's repair approach as a 34-year-old programmer: "After arguments, I need explicit reassurance that we're okay and that my girlfriend still loves me despite seeing me dysregulated. She needs acknowledgment that her feelings were valid even if I was overwhelmed. Our repair ritual includes both of those things plus a specific plan for handling similar triggers differently. It takes about 30 minutes but prevents arguments from damaging our relationship long-term."

Learning from patterns: Conflict as information

Instead of viewing conflicts as relationship failures, you can use them as information about your triggers, needs, and areas for growth. AuDHD brains are excellent at pattern recognition when given the right tools and frameworks.

Conflict pattern analysis for AuDHD:

Trigger identification: What situations, topics, or stressors typically lead to conflict? **Escalation tracking:** How do your conflicts usually develop and intensify? **Response patterns:** How do you typically react during different types of disagreements? **Resolution effectiveness:** Which strategies work for resolving conflicts versus which ones make things worse? **Aftermath patterns:** How do you both typically feel and behave after conflicts end?

Creating your conflict profile:

Environmental triggers: Times of day, locations, or sensory factors that increase conflict likelihood **Emotional triggers:** Rejection sensitivity, overwhelm, or specific relationship fears that escalate disagreements **Communication triggers:** Misunderstandings, processing differences, or unmet needs that spark arguments **External triggers:** Work stress, family issues, or life changes that affect your conflict patterns **Neurological triggers:** Low energy, sensory overload, or executive function struggles that increase conflict risk

Using patterns for prevention:

Once you identify your conflict patterns, you can develop prevention strategies:

- Avoid discussing emotional topics during high-trigger times
- Create environmental modifications that reduce conflict likelihood
- Develop early intervention strategies when you notice escalation beginning
- Build in extra support during times when conflicts are more likely
- Practice specific skills for your most common conflict patterns

Consider Rachel's pattern analysis as a 29-year-old therapist: "I realized that 90% of our conflicts happen on Sunday evenings when I'm anxious about the upcoming week and my boyfriend is tired from social activities. Now we have a Sunday evening routine that includes separate alone time and postponing serious conversations until Monday evening. We've cut our conflicts by about 80% just by recognizing this pattern."

Practical Conflict Tools

Conflict Style Assessment for AuDHD

Identify your personal conflict patterns:

During conflicts, I typically:

- Become hyperverbal and over-explain my position
- Shut down and become unable to communicate
- Get emotionally flooded and can't think logically
- Bring up past issues and examples
- Need to leave the room or environment
- Become focused on being "right" rather than resolving the issue

My biggest conflict triggers are:

- Feeling misunderstood or invalidated
- Sensory overwhelm during emotional conversations
- Time pressure to resolve issues quickly
- Feeling like my partner is angry or disappointed with me
- Conflicts during times when I'm already stressed
- Discussions that involve multiple complex topics

What helps me during conflicts:

- Taking breaks to process emotions and thoughts
- Written communication instead of verbal discussion
- Clear, direct feedback rather than hints or implications
- Reassurance about the relationship during disagreements
- Environmental modifications like dimmer lighting or quieter spaces
- Specific examples rather than general complaints

Customizable Conflict Pause Cards

Create cards to use during heated moments:

Card 1: "Processing Pause" "I need time to process my emotions and organize my thoughts. Let's continue this conversation in [timeframe]. This pause helps me communicate effectively, not avoid the issue."

Card 2: "Sensory Break" "I'm getting sensory overload which is affecting my ability to focus on our conversation. I need to modify our environment or take a break to regulate my nervous system."

Card 3: "Meltdown Protocol" "I'm approaching meltdown and need to focus on regulation right now. We'll return to this conversation when I'm safe and regulated."

Card 4: "Clarification Request" "I'm having trouble following this conversation. Can we slow down and make sure I understand what you're saying before we continue?"

Post-Conflict Debrief Template

Use this structure for learning from conflicts:

What happened:

- What was the original trigger or issue?
- How did the conflict escalate?
- What made it difficult to resolve?

What each person experienced:

- How did I feel during the conflict?
- What was my partner's experience?
- Where did our communication break down?

What worked:

- Which strategies helped de-escalate the situation?
- What communication approaches were effective?
- How did we successfully reconnect afterward?

What to change:

- What would I do differently next time?
- What environmental or timing factors could we modify?
- Which skills do we need to practice for similar situations?

Prevention planning:

- How can we catch this pattern earlier next time?
- What support does each person need during similar conflicts?
- What agreements do we want to make about this type of issue?

Building Your Conflict Resilience

Conflict in AuDHD relationships doesn't have to be destructive or overwhelming. With understanding of how your neurology affects disagreements and specific strategies that work with your brain rather than against it, you can develop approaches that actually strengthen your relationship through conflict resolution.

The goal isn't to eliminate all conflicts—it's to navigate them safely while building deeper understanding and connection. Your neurological differences can actually become strengths in conflict resolution when you develop appropriate tools and frameworks.

This foundation of healthy conflict navigation becomes especially important as you address the next crucial aspect of AuDHD relationships: managing your energy as a finite resource. Understanding how conflicts drain your energy helps you plan better, while energy management skills help you prevent conflicts that stem from overwhelm and depletion.

Building Blocks for Healthy Disagreements

- AuDHD creates unique conflict experiences requiring specialized strategies beyond standard relationship advice
- Adapted STOP protocols provide safety and processing time that honor neurological needs
- Meltdowns during conflict require immediate safety focus rather than continued discussion
- Extended time-outs support the processing differences inherent in AuDHD neurology
- Repair rituals and pattern analysis transform conflicts into relationship growth opportunities

Chapter 10: Managing energy as a finite resource

You wake up feeling ready to tackle the day, but by 2 PM you're completely drained. A simple conversation with your partner about weekend plans feels overwhelming. The grocery store trip you planned seems impossible. You haven't even done anything particularly strenuous, but your energy reserves are completely depleted.

This is the reality of living with an AuDHD brain—your energy is finite and gets used up faster than most people realize. Every social interaction, sensory experience, and executive function task withdraws from your limited energy account. Meanwhile, traditional relationship advice assumes unlimited energy for communication, social activities, and emotional processing.

Understanding energy management in AuDHD relationships changes everything about how you approach daily life together. Instead of pushing through exhaustion and burning out, you can learn to budget your energy like any other limited resource and create sustainable relationship rhythms that work with your neurology.

The energy economy: Why you have less than you think

Research from Autism Spectrum News confirms that neurodivergent individuals experience faster energy depletion due to the additional cognitive load required for social interaction, sensory processing, and executive function management. Your brain is constantly working harder than neurotypical brains to navigate the same daily experiences.

Hidden energy drains in AuDHD:

Masking costs: Suppressing stimming, forcing eye contact, and following social scripts requires constant energy **Sensory processing:** Your brain works overtime to filter and manage sensory input throughout the day **Executive function load:** Planning, organizing, and managing daily tasks uses more mental energy than for neurotypical brains **Social translation:** Converting your thoughts into socially acceptable communication depletes cognitive resources **Emotional regulation:** Managing intense emotions and rejection sensitivity requires significant energy expenditure

The compound effect:

Each energy drain might seem manageable individually, but they compound throughout the day. By evening, you might feel completely exhausted despite not doing anything that would tire a neurotypical person.

Consider Jake's daily energy tracking as a 33-year-old librarian: "I started logging my energy levels hourly and realized I was losing energy constantly throughout the day, not just during obviously draining activities. A five-minute conversation with a coworker cost me energy. Walking through the busy library affected my energy. Even choosing what to eat for lunch used up mental resources. By the time I got home to my boyfriend, I had nothing left for our relationship."

Jake's experience illustrates how AuDHD energy depletion happens gradually and invisibly, making it difficult to understand why you feel so exhausted by everyday activities.

Energy types affected by AuDHD:

Social energy: Capacity for interaction, conversation, and emotional connection **Sensory energy:** Ability to tolerate and process environmental stimuli **Cognitive energy:** Mental resources for thinking, problem-solving, and decision-making **Emotional energy:** Capacity for processing feelings and managing emotional responses **Physical energy:** Bodily resources for movement, activity, and physical presence

Spoon theory meets relationships: Budgeting connection

Spoon theory, developed by Christine Miserandino, explains how people with chronic illness have limited energy "spoons" each day. This concept applies perfectly to AuDHD relationships—you have limited energy spoons for social connection, and once they're used up, you need time to replenish.

Applying spoon theory to relationships:

Morning assessment: Check how many spoons you have available for relationship activities **Activity planning:** Estimate spoon cost for different relationship interactions **Spoon monitoring:** Track energy depletion throughout the day **Reserve management:** Keep emergency spoons for unexpected relationship needs **Recovery planning:** Schedule spoon replenishment time

Relationship activity spoon costs:

Low-cost activities (1-2 spoons):

- Watching movies together in silence
- Parallel activities like reading in the same room
- Brief check-ins about daily logistics
- Physical affection without conversation

Medium-cost activities (3-4 spoons):

- Normal conversations about feelings or experiences
- Social activities with familiar people
- Planning future activities together
- Household management discussions

High-cost activities (5+ spoons):

- Emotional conflicts or difficult conversations
- Large social gatherings or parties
- Meeting new people or dating activities
- Major decision-making discussions

Emergency situations (variable costs):

- Unexpected relationship crises
- Partner having emotional difficulties
- Family emergencies or sudden changes
- Conflicts that require immediate attention

Maria, a 30-year-old social worker, explains her spoon budgeting: "I wake up with about 12 relationship spoons each day. Work uses up 6-8 spoons, so I come home with 4-6 left for my girlfriend. If she wants to discuss something important, that might use 5 spoons, leaving me with almost nothing. Now we plan emotional conversations for weekends when I start with more spoons and haven't used them all at work."

Energy drains vs. fills: Identifying your patterns

Not all activities drain energy—some actually restore it. Understanding your personal energy drains versus energy fills helps you design relationship activities that sustain rather than deplete you.

Common AuDHD energy drains:

Social performance: Maintaining conversation, reading social cues, managing your presentation to others **Sensory overwhelm:** Crowded places, loud environments, bright lights, strong smells **Emotional intensity:** Processing your own or your partner's strong emotions **Executive function demands:** Planning activities, making decisions, managing schedules **Novelty and unpredictability:** New environments, unexpected changes, unfamiliar social situations

Common AuDHD energy fills:

Special interest engagement: Activities related to your passionate interests **Sensory regulation:** Pleasant sensory experiences like weighted blankets, preferred music, or comfortable textures **Predictable routines:** Familiar activities that don't require decision-making or adaptation **Authentic connection:** Conversations or activities where you can be completely yourself **Solitude and**

processing time: Alone time to recharge your social and sensory systems

Individual variation in energy patterns:

What drains one AuDHD person might fill another. You need to identify your specific patterns rather than assuming general rules apply to you.

Creating your energy profile:

Track your energy levels for several weeks, noting:

- Which activities consistently drain you
- Which activities restore your energy
- How different types of social interaction affect you
- What time of day you have most/least energy
- How external factors like stress or hormones affect your energy patterns

David, a 32-year-old engineer, discovered his unique energy patterns: "I assumed all social interaction drained me, but I realized that's not true. Talking about engineering problems with my girlfriend actually gives me energy because it's my special interest and she's genuinely curious. But small talk at parties completely exhausts me. Understanding this difference helped us plan social activities that work with my energy instead of against it."

The recharge imperative: Alone time without guilt

AuDHD individuals typically need more alone time than neurotypical people realize. This isn't antisocial behavior or relationship rejection—it's neurological maintenance required for healthy functioning.

Why AuDHD brains need alone time:

Sensory recovery: Time without stimulating input allows your sensory system to reset **Social processing:** Space to analyze and integrate social experiences without new input **Emotional regulation:** Opportunity to process feelings without managing others' emotions simultaneously **Cognitive restoration:** Mental break from the constant work of social navigation **Authentic expression:** Freedom to stim, vocalize, or behave naturally without social performance

Communicating alone time needs:

Many partners interpret requests for alone time as rejection or relationship problems. Clear communication about the neurological basis for these needs prevents misunderstanding.

Scripts for explaining alone time needs:

"I need alone time to recharge my nervous system, not because I don't want to be with you. Think of it like plugging in a phone that's running low on battery."

"My brain works differently and gets overwhelmed by constant social input. Alone time helps me regulate so I can be fully present when we're together."

"This isn't about you or our relationship. My neurology requires processing time to function well. I'll be much better company after I recharge."

Creating sustainable alone time:

Daily micro-recharges: 15-30 minutes of solitude during busy days
Weekly extended recharges: 2-4 hours of uninterrupted alone time
Monthly deep recharges: Half or full days without social obligations
Emergency recharges: Permission to take alone time when unexpectedly overwhelmed

Sarah, a 28-year-old teacher, established her recharge routine: "I need 45 minutes of alone time when I get home from work before I can engage with my husband. At first, he thought I was avoiding him or didn't want to see him. Now he understands it's like letting a computer restart—I need that processing time to be fully present for our evening together. He uses that time for his own activities, and then we both get the best versions of each other."

Syncing energy cycles: When partners' needs conflict

Managing energy becomes more complex when both partners have different energy patterns or when one partner's energy needs conflict with the other's. Creating systems that honor both people's energy requirements prevents resentment and exhaustion.

Common energy conflicts in relationships:

Mismatched energy timing: One partner wants connection when the other needs alone time **Different energy capacities:** One partner has significantly more or less social energy than the other **Competing energy needs:** Both partners need support simultaneously but neither has capacity to give **External energy demands:** Work, family, or social obligations that drain energy needed for the relationship **Energy emergency conflicts:** Crisis situations that require energy neither partner has available

Energy syncing strategies:

Communicate energy levels: Share daily energy assessments so both partners know current capacity **Plan energy-intensive activities:** Schedule high-demand relationship activities for high-energy times **Create energy flexibility:** Build buffer time around energy-draining activities **Develop support networks:** Have other sources of support beyond your partner for emotional or practical needs **Practice energy conservation:** Modify activities to reduce energy costs when possible

The energy checking system:

Develop a simple way to communicate current energy levels:

Green energy: Full capacity for social interaction and relationship activities **Yellow energy:** Limited capacity, prefer low-demand activities **Red energy:** Minimal capacity, need mostly alone time or very gentle interaction **Emergency mode:** No capacity for relationship demands, need full support and recovery time

Lisa, a 31-year-old nurse, describes her energy syncing with her partner: "We both have ADHD and autism, so our energy patterns are different but we both understand the experience. We check in each morning about our energy colors for the day. If we're both red or yellow, we plan a low-key evening. If one of us is green and the other is red, the green person handles more of the household stuff while the red person rests. It prevents conflicts about who should do what based on current capacity rather than arbitrary fairness."

Emergency reserves: Planning for low-energy periods

Life inevitably includes periods when your energy is severely depleted—during illness, major stress, life transitions, or autistic burnout. Having emergency protocols prevents these periods from damaging your relationship.

Preparing for energy emergencies:

Identify warning signs: Learn to recognize when you're approaching energy depletion before crisis hits **Create emergency protocols:** Establish specific plans for how to handle low-energy periods **Build support networks:** Develop resources beyond your partner for practical and emotional support **Modify expectations:** Adjust relationship maintenance activities during low-energy times **Plan recovery strategies:** Know what helps you restore energy most effectively

Emergency energy protocols:

Immediate needs assessment: What are the absolute minimum requirements for safety and basic functioning? **Task delegation:** Which responsibilities can be temporarily handled by others? **Energy**

conservation: What activities can be eliminated or modified to preserve energy? **Recovery timeline:** How long do you typically need to restore normal energy levels? **Support mobilization:** Who can provide help with practical tasks, emotional support, or professional guidance?

Low-energy relationship modifications:

Communication simplification: Switch to text or written communication instead of verbal conversation **Activity reduction:** Focus only on essential relationship maintenance, postpone optional activities **Increased independence:** Both partners handle their own needs more independently temporarily **External support utilization:** Rely more heavily on friends, family, or professional help **Expectations adjustment:** Accept that relationship functioning will be different during recovery

Michael, a 34-year-old programmer, developed his emergency energy plan: "During my autistic burnout last year, I couldn't handle normal relationship activities for about three months. My girlfriend and I had already discussed this possibility and created a plan. She took over most household management, we communicated mainly through texts, and I focused entirely on recovery. Having the plan in place meant we didn't have to make decisions about what to do while I was already overwhelmed."

Practical Energy Management Tools

Daily Energy Tracking System

Create a simple method for monitoring energy throughout the day:

Morning energy assessment: Rate your starting energy level on a 1-10 scale for:

- Social interaction capacity
- Sensory tolerance level
- Cognitive function availability

- Emotional processing capacity
- Physical energy reserves

Hourly check-ins: Note significant energy changes and what caused them:

- Energy draining activities or experiences
- Energy restoring moments or activities
- Environmental factors affecting energy
- Physical or emotional factors influencing capacity

Evening energy review: Assess your ending energy levels and plan recovery:

- What drained the most energy today?
- What restored energy effectively?
- How much recovery time do you need tonight?
- What's your predicted energy for tomorrow?

Energy Budget Planner for Couples

Plan relationship activities based on available energy:

Weekly energy planning:

- Identify high and low energy days for both partners
- Schedule energy-intensive activities during high-capacity times
- Plan low-key connection activities for low-energy periods
- Build in recovery time after energy-draining activities

Daily energy budgeting:

- Morning energy check-in for both partners
- Adjust daily plans based on current capacity
- Identify who has more energy for household or relationship tasks
- Plan evening activities based on remaining energy levels

Emergency energy protocols:

- Signs that energy reserves are critically low
- Immediate modifications to reduce energy demands
- Support person contact information and availability
- Recovery timeline and monitoring plan

Recharge Activity Menu Creator

Develop personalized lists of energy-restoring activities:

5-minute recharges:

- Brief stimming or movement
- Listening to favorite music with headphones
- Looking at special interest content
- Deep breathing or brief meditation

15-30 minute recharges:

- Shower or bath with preferred temperature and lighting
- Engaging with special interest materials
- Gentle movement or stretching
- Creative activities like drawing or writing

1-2 hour recharges:

- Complete solitude in comfortable environment
- Immersive special interest activities
- Preferred sensory experiences
- Restorative sleep or rest

Half or full day recharges:

- Complete schedule clearing with no obligations
- Extended special interest engagement
- Minimal social interaction requirements
- Full environmental control and sensory optimization

Quick Energy Boosts for Couples

Low-energy connection activities:

- Watching familiar shows or movies together silently
- Parallel activities like reading in the same room
- Brief physical affection without conversation expectations
- Sharing special interest content without discussion pressure

Partner energy support:

- Taking over household tasks when partner is depleted
- Providing sensory comfort like weighted blankets or preferred lighting
- Maintaining quiet environment for recovery
- Handling external social or family obligations independently

Creating Your Energy-Aware Relationship

Energy management in AuDHD relationships requires ongoing attention and adjustment, but it prevents the burnout and resentment that come from constantly operating beyond your capacity. Understanding energy as a finite resource helps you make conscious choices about how to spend it rather than accidentally depleting yourself.

The goal isn't to have unlimited energy—it's to work with your actual energy levels to create sustainable relationship patterns. This awareness becomes especially important as you address the next aspect of AuDHD relationships: building routines that provide structure while allowing for the flexibility your brain needs.

Effective energy management creates the foundation for sustainable routines, while good routines help preserve and restore your energy more efficiently.

Energy Management Essentials

- AuDHD brains have finite energy that depletes faster due to masking, sensory processing, and executive function demands
- Spoon theory helps budget relationship activities based on available energy capacity
- Individual energy drain and fill patterns require personal tracking rather than general assumptions
- Alone time is neurological maintenance, not relationship avoidance or antisocial behavior
- Emergency energy protocols prevent low-capacity periods from damaging relationship stability

Chapter 11: Building routines that flex

Your autism brain craves the security of routine—knowing what to expect, when to expect it, and how each day will unfold. But your ADHD brain rebels against rigid structure, seeking novelty, spontaneity, and the freedom to follow interesting impulses. This neurological tug-of-war affects every aspect of your relationship, from daily schedules to vacation planning.

Traditional advice suggests either strict routines for autism or complete flexibility for ADHD, but neither approach works when you have both conditions. You need something different: flexible frameworks that provide enough structure to feel secure while allowing enough variation to stay engaged.

Research from The Conversation shows that individuals with co-occurring autism and ADHD face unique challenges in routine development because their needs seem contradictory. But these needs aren't actually opposite—they're different aspects of the same desire for optimal functioning.

The routine paradox: Structure vs. spontaneity needs

The conflict between structure and spontaneity creates daily stress in AuDHD relationships. Your partner might not understand why you need detailed plans for some activities but resist scheduling others. You might feel equally frustrated by too much structure and not enough predictability.

How autism drives routine needs:

Predictability reduces anxiety by eliminating uncertainty about daily events **Consistent patterns support executive function** by reducing decision-making demands **Familiar sequences feel safe** because you know what's expected and how to respond **Detailed planning prevents overwhelm** by breaking complex activities into manageable steps **Routine maintenance provides control** in a world that often feels chaotic and unpredictable

How ADHD disrupts routine adherence:

Novelty-seeking creates boredom with repetitive patterns and unchanging schedules **Impulsivity leads to spontaneous changes** that disrupt carefully planned routines **Hyperfocus causes time blindness** that makes you miss scheduled activities or transitions **Executive function challenges affect consistency** in maintaining routines even when you want them **Emotional variations change needs** so routines that work on good days don't work during difficult periods

The paradox in relationships:

These opposing needs create scenarios where you simultaneously crave and resist routine. You might plan a detailed weekend schedule then feel trapped by it. You might enjoy spontaneous date nights but feel anxious without knowing what to expect.

Consider Tom's experience as a 35-year-old accountant: "I need our morning routine to be exactly the same every day—coffee, shower, check emails in that order. But if we do the same thing for dinner three nights in a row, I feel like I'm suffocating. My girlfriend gets confused because sometimes I seem to love routine and other times I seem to hate it. I'm not being inconsistent—different parts of my day have different flexibility needs."

Tom's experience illustrates how routine needs vary across different life areas and times. Understanding these variations helps create flexible systems rather than rigid rules.

Flexible frameworks: Routines that bend without breaking

Instead of fixed routines, AuDHD relationships benefit from flexible frameworks—structured approaches that provide predictability while allowing for variation and spontaneity within defined parameters.

Elements of flexible frameworks:

Core constants: Non-negotiable elements that remain the same for security **Variable components:** Aspects that can change within established boundaries **Choice points:** Predetermined moments where spontaneous decisions are welcome **Escape clauses:** Built-in options for modifying or abandoning plans when needed **Recovery protocols:** Systems for returning to routine after disruptions

Examples of flexible frameworks:

Morning routine framework:

- Core constant: Wake up time and first activity (coffee/medication)
- Variable component: Order of getting ready activities
- Choice point: What to wear based on mood and weather
- Escape clause: Simplified routine for low-energy days

Evening routine framework:

- Core constant: Transition time between work and home life
- Variable component: Specific relaxation activities chosen daily
- Choice point: Dinner timing and preparation method
- Escape clause: Takeout option for overwhelming days

Weekend framework:

- Core constant: One structured activity and one completely unscheduled block
- Variable component: Which structured activity based on current interests
- Choice point: Spontaneous activities during unscheduled time
- Escape clause: Complete schedule clearing for energy recovery

Date night framework:

- Core constant: Regular timing (every Saturday evening)

- Variable component: Activity type rotated monthly (home dates, outings, adventures)
- Choice point: Specific activity chosen day-of based on energy and mood
- Escape clause: Low-key backup plan for overwhelming periods

Sarah, a 29-year-old therapist, developed flexible frameworks with her partner: "We have breakfast together every morning—that's our core constant. But sometimes it's elaborate cooking, sometimes it's cereal, sometimes it's going out. The constant is the together time, not the specific activity. This gives my autism brain the predictability it needs while giving my ADHD brain the variety it craves."

Transition strategies: Moving between activities smoothly

Transitions—moving from one activity to another—pose particular challenges for AuDHD individuals. Your autism brain needs time to process endings and beginnings. Your ADHD brain might hyperfocus on current activities and struggle to shift attention.

Why transitions are challenging for AuDHD:

Task switching difficulties make it hard to stop current activities and start new ones **Time blindness** creates problems with estimating transition duration and planning accordingly **Hyperfocus intensity** makes interrupting engaging activities feel jarring or frustrating **Processing time needs** require space to mentally prepare for upcoming activities **Sensory adjustments** needed when moving between different environments or activity types

Transition strategy framework:

Warning systems: Multiple alerts before transitions need to happen **Bridge activities:** Small actions that connect current activity to next activity **Processing buffers:** Built-in time for mental adjustment between activities **Environmental preparation:** Setting up spaces for upcoming activities in advance **Energy assessment:** Checking capacity before committing to transition timing

Practical transition protocols:

15-minute warning: "In 15 minutes, we'll need to start getting ready to leave" **5-minute bridge:** "Let's start winding down this activity and thinking about what's next" **Transition moment:** "Now we're switching to getting ready mode" **Environmental shift:** Moving to appropriate space and gathering needed items **Activity initiation:** Beginning new activity with clear first step

Relationship transition applications:

Work to home transition: Buffer time between ending work activities and engaging in relationship activities **Social to alone transition:** Processing time after social activities before engaging in intimate conversation **Conflict to connection transition:** Repair time after disagreements before returning to normal relationship activities **Weekend to weekday transition:** Gradual shift from relaxed weekend routines to structured weekday patterns

Michael, a 33-year-old librarian, uses transition strategies in his relationship: "My boyfriend learned that I can't go straight from work mode to relationship mode. I need 20 minutes to transition—change clothes, have a snack, maybe stim a little. He uses that time for his own transition activities. Then we can actually connect instead of me being overwhelmed and him feeling ignored."

The novelty injection: Planned spontaneity that works

AuDHD brains need novelty and variety, but completely unpredictable spontaneity can trigger anxiety and overwhelm. Planned spontaneity provides novelty within safe, predictable frameworks.

Principles of planned spontaneity:

Scheduled flexibility: Specific times designated for spontaneous decisions **Bounded choices:** Multiple options within acceptable parameters **Safety nets:** Backup plans if spontaneous choices don't work out **Energy consideration:** Spontaneity planned for high-energy times, not when depleted **Partner preparation:** Both people prepared for and consenting to spontaneous elements

Planned spontaneity strategies:

Choice menus: Pre-approved lists of activities to choose from spontaneously **Adventure budgets:** Designated time and resources for unplanned activities **Exploration windows:** Specific times set aside for trying new things without pressure **Surprise protocols:** Agreed-upon ways partners can introduce pleasant surprises **Discovery dates:** Planned times for exploring new places or activities together

Examples of successful planned spontaneity:

Dinner roulette: List of 10 acceptable restaurants, roll dice to choose **Activity jar:** Collection of date ideas to draw from when feeling spontaneous **Weekend adventure:** Saturday morning decision about day trips within 2-hour drive **Learning exploration:** Monthly choice to explore new topic or skill together **Seasonal variety:** Different activity categories for different times of year

Lisa, a 31-year-old nurse, explains her planned spontaneity system: "We have a jar full of date ideas that we add to regularly. On Friday nights, we draw one out and do whatever it says on Saturday. It feels spontaneous because we don't know what we'll pick, but it's safe because everything in the jar is something we've both agreed we want to try. It satisfies my ADHD need for novelty and my autism need for predictable safety."

When routines fail: Recovery without shame

Routines will inevitably break down due to illness, stress, life changes, or simple human limitations. AuDHD individuals often experience shame and anxiety when routines fail, feeling like personal failures rather than normal life variations.

Common routine failure triggers:

External disruptions: Illness, travel, family emergencies, work demands **Internal changes:** Energy fluctuations, seasonal affects, hormonal changes, medication adjustments **Relationship factors:** Partner schedule changes, conflict aftermath, major decisions **Life transitions:** Moving, job changes, family additions, loss or grief **Capacity limits:** Attempting more than energy or executive function can sustain

Routine failure recovery strategies:

Normalize the experience: Routine disruption is normal and temporary, not personal failure **Assess current capacity:** Determine what level of routine is sustainable right now **Simplify temporarily:** Strip routines down to absolute essentials during recovery **Gradual rebuilding:** Add routine elements back slowly rather than attempting full restoration immediately **Adjust expectations:** Modify routines based on current life circumstances rather than forcing previous patterns

Recovery protocols for routine breakdown:

Immediate stabilization: Focus on basic needs and essential daily structure **Capacity assessment:** Evaluate current energy and executive function availability **Priority identification:** Determine which routine elements are most important for functioning **Simplified implementation:** Create bare-minimum version of essential routines **Gradual expansion:** Slowly add routine elements as capacity increases

Preventing shame spirals during routine breakdown:

Reframe setbacks as information: What do routine failures tell you about your needs and limits? **Practice self-compassion:** Treat yourself with kindness during difficult adjustment periods **Seek**

support: Allow partner and others to help maintain essential routines temporarily **Focus on values:** Maintain routines that support your core values and let go of others temporarily **Plan for flexibility:** Build routine breakdown recovery into your normal expectations

David, a 32-year-old engineer, describes his routine recovery approach: "When my dad died last year, all our routines fell apart for months. Instead of trying to force our normal schedule, my wife and I created a grief routine—much simpler but still providing structure. Morning coffee together, brief evening check-ins, and one planned activity each weekend. As we healed, we gradually added back other routine elements. It took almost a year to return to our previous routines, but the simplified version kept us connected during crisis."

Seasonal adjustments: Adapting to life changes

AuDHD routine needs change with seasons, life stages, relationship development, and external circumstances. Building routine flexibility means expecting and planning for these changes rather than viewing them as disruptions.

Factors requiring routine adjustments:

Seasonal changes: Different light levels, temperatures, and activity options affecting routine preferences **Relationship evolution:** Growing intimacy, changing needs, and developing shared interests requiring routine modification **Life stage transitions:** Career changes, family development, aging, and health changes affecting routine capacity **External environment shifts:** Moving, schedule changes, social circle evolution, and community involvement changes

Adjustment strategies for routine evolution:

Regular routine reviews: Scheduled times to assess what's working and what needs modification **Experimental periods:** Trying new routine elements temporarily before committing to changes **Gradual modifications:** Making small adjustments rather than complete routine overhauls **Feedback integration:** Using partner input and personal experience to refine routine choices **Flexibility planning:** Building change capacity into routine expectations

Seasonal routine adaptation examples:

Summer routines: Later bedtimes, more outdoor activities, vacation considerations **Winter routines:** Earlier evenings, indoor focus, seasonal affective considerations **Holiday routines:** Temporary modifications for family obligations and social expectations **Anniversary routines:** Special relationship maintenance during significant dates

Rachel, a 28-year-old social worker, adapts her routines seasonally: "Our morning routine completely changes between summer and winter. Summer mornings include outdoor time and lighter meals. Winter mornings focus on light therapy and warming activities. We review and adjust our routines every three months to make sure they still fit our current needs and circumstances."

Practical Routine Building Tools

Flexible Routine Builder Worksheet

Design routines with built-in flexibility:

Core Constants (non-negotiable elements):

- Which activities must happen for security and functioning?
- What timing or sequence is essential for success?
- Which environmental factors are required for comfort?

Variable Components (changeable elements):

- Which activities can be modified while maintaining core purpose?
- What choices can be made daily or weekly within routine structure?

- Which elements can be simplified or expanded based on energy?

Choice Points (scheduled spontaneity):

- Where in the routine can spontaneous decisions be made?
- What boundaries keep choices manageable and safe?
- How much time is needed for choice-making without pressure?

Escape Clauses (modification options):

- What triggers indicate routine modification is needed?
- What simplified versions can maintain essential elements?
- How can routines be paused and resumed without guilt?

Transition Ritual Creator

Develop smooth movement between activities:

Warning system design:

- How much advance notice do you need for activity changes?
- What types of reminders work best for your brain?
- Who is responsible for providing transition warnings?

Bridge activity identification:

- What small actions help you mentally shift between activities?
- Which preparatory steps ease transition anxiety?
- How can you honor the ending of current activities?

Processing buffer planning:

- How much time do you need between activities?
- What helps you prepare mentally for upcoming activities?
- Which environmental changes support smooth transitions?

Routine Modification Protocol

Systematic approach for changing routines:

Assessment phase:

- What aspects of current routines are working well?
- Which elements create stress, boredom, or dysfunction?
- What external factors require routine adjustments?

Experimental design:

- What small changes can be tested without major disruption?
- How long will you try modifications before evaluating success?
- What criteria will determine if changes should be permanent?

Implementation strategy:

- How will routine changes be introduced gradually?
- What support is needed during transition periods?
- How will both partners adapt to routine modifications?

Evaluation and refinement:

- How will you track the success of routine changes?
- What adjustments might be needed after initial implementation?
- When will you schedule the next routine review session?

Micro-Routines for Macro-Impact

Small routine elements that create significant benefits:

Connection micro-routines:

- 30-second morning greeting ritual
- Brief evening gratitude sharing

- Weekly relationship check-in timing
- Daily physical affection moment

Transition micro-routines:

- Specific phrase or action that signals activity changes
- Brief pause between activities for mental preparation
- Environmental reset actions (turning off lights, clearing surfaces)
- Physical movement that helps brain shift focus

Recovery micro-routines:

- Five-minute reset routine for overwhelming moments
- Brief recovery ritual after difficult conversations
- Daily wind-down sequence for better sleep
- Weekly energy restoration practice

Building Your Relationship Rhythm

Flexible routines in AuDHD relationships require ongoing attention and adjustment, but they provide the structure your autism brain needs while honoring the variety your ADHD brain craves. The goal isn't perfect routine adherence—it's creating frameworks that support both partners' functioning while building connection.

These flexible frameworks become especially important as you navigate social situations and external relationships that can either support or drain your carefully crafted routines. Understanding how to protect your routine and energy while engaging with the broader social world helps maintain the stability you've built together.

The next aspect of AuDHD relationships involves managing your social life as a couple while maintaining boundaries that protect your individual and relationship needs.

Routine Building Foundations

- AuDHD needs both structure for security and flexibility for engagement, requiring frameworks rather than rigid routines
- Flexible frameworks provide core constants while allowing variable components and choice points
- Transition strategies help navigate activity changes without overwhelming your nervous system
- Planned spontaneity satisfies novelty needs within safe, predictable parameters
- Routine failures are normal life events requiring recovery strategies, not shame or self-criticism

Chapter 12: Social life and couple boundaries

The wedding invitation arrives with a plus-one, but you already feel overwhelmed just reading about the cocktail hour, dinner service, and dancing. Your partner sees a fun celebration with friends. You see sensory overwhelm, social performance pressure, and energy depletion that will take days to recover from. Meanwhile, you're both trying to maintain friendships, family relationships, and social connections that seem designed for neurotypical brains.

This is the ongoing challenge of AuDHD social life—balancing your need for connection with your neurological limitations, while maintaining relationships that matter to both of you. Your social energy is limited, your sensory capacity is finite, and your masking ability has limits. But isolation isn't the answer either.

Creating sustainable social boundaries as an AuDHD couple requires careful navigation between social obligations and self-preservation, between maintaining relationships and protecting your energy, between appearing "normal" and honoring your authentic needs.

The social energy equation: When partners have different needs

Social energy calculations become complex when partners have different neurological profiles, social preferences, or family obligations. You might need hours of recovery time after social events while your partner feels energized by the same activities. Or you might both be introverted but have different tolerance levels for various social situations.

Common social energy mismatches:

Introvert/extravert differences: One partner gains energy from social interaction while the other depletes quickly **Sensory tolerance variations:** Different levels of tolerance for crowds, noise, or stimulating environments **Masking costs:** One partner expends significant energy on social performance while the other operates more naturally **Family obligation differences:** Varying levels of family social demands and expectations **Recovery time needs:** Different requirements for alone time or low-stimulation periods after social activities

Creating equitable social energy agreements:

Individual energy assessment: Both partners understand their own social energy patterns and limitations **Communication systems:** Clear ways to express current social capacity and needs **Shared decision-making:** Collaborative approaches to social commitments that consider both partners' needs **Support strategies:** Ways partners can help each other during and after challenging social situations **Recovery planning:** Built-in time and space for social energy restoration

Consider Emma's experience as a 27-year-old teacher: "My husband loves parties and gets energy from being around lots of people. I get completely drained after an hour of small talk and need two days to recover. We used to fight about social invitations because he thought I was being antisocial and I thought he didn't understand my limitations. Now we have agreements—he can go to events alone sometimes, I can leave early when we go together, and we always plan recovery time after social activities."

Emma's approach demonstrates how different social needs can be accommodated through explicit agreements rather than forcing one partner to adapt to the other's preferences.

Social energy budgeting for couples:

Weekly social planning: Assessing upcoming social demands and planning energy accordingly **Event evaluation:** Considering energy cost versus relationship benefit for each social commitment **Recovery scheduling:** Building in appropriate restoration time after energy-intensive social activities **Flexibility planning:** Creating backup plans for when social energy is lower than expected

Boundary setting with others: Protecting couple time

External social pressures can overwhelm AuDHD individuals and relationships. Well-meaning friends and family members might not understand your need for advance notice, limited social time, or specific environmental accommodations. Learning to set boundaries protects your relationship while maintaining important connections.

Common boundary challenges:

Last-minute invitations: Pressure to attend events without adequate preparation time **Extended social obligations:** Events that exceed your social energy capacity **Unwelcome advice:** Others offering suggestions about "overcoming" your social limitations **Guilt manipulation:** Emotional pressure about being "antisocial" or "high-maintenance" **Environmental demands:** Social situations in sensory-overwhelming or uncomfortable settings

Boundary-setting strategies for AuDHD couples:

Clear communication: Direct statements about your needs rather than vague excuses **Advance planning:** Requiring notice for social commitments to plan energy and preparation **Time limits:** Setting specific durations for social activities based on your capacity **Environmental modifications:** Requesting or creating accommodations that support your participation **Alternative suggestions:** Offering different ways to connect that work better for your needs

Sample boundary scripts:

For advance notice needs: "We need at least a week's notice for social plans so we can manage our energy and schedules effectively."

For time limitations: "We'd love to join you for dinner, but we'll need to leave by 8 PM due to our evening routine."

For environmental accommodations: "We can come to the party, but we'll need to step outside periodically if the noise level gets overwhelming."

For declining invitations: "That sounds fun, but it's not a good fit for our energy levels right now. Could we get together for coffee next week instead?"

For persistent pressure: "I understand you want us to be more social, but we need to manage our activities based on our neurological needs. This isn't negotiable."

Research from The Other Autism emphasizes the importance of neurodivergent individuals finding and maintaining community connections that understand and accommodate their needs, rather than forcing themselves into unsuitable social expectations.

The explanation dilemma: How much to disclose socially

Deciding how much to share about your AuDHD needs with friends, family, and acquaintances requires careful consideration. Too little information leads to misunderstanding and judgment. Too much information can feel overwhelming for others or invite unwanted advice.

Factors affecting disclosure decisions:

Relationship closeness: How well you know the person and how much you trust them **Context requirements:** How much information is needed for the situation to work **Safety considerations:** Your emotional and social safety in the relationship **Energy availability:** Your current capacity for education and advocacy **Support potential:** The person's likely response and ability to provide appropriate accommodation

Disclosure levels for different relationships:

Minimal disclosure (acquaintances, casual friends): "I have some sensory sensitivities that affect social situations" **Moderate disclosure (close friends, regular social contacts):** "I'm autistic and have ADHD, which means I need some accommodations for social activities" **Full disclosure (very close friends, chosen family):** Detailed explanation of specific needs, triggers, and support strategies

Strategic disclosure approaches:

Need-based sharing: Sharing only information relevant to current situation **Educational framing:** Positioning disclosure as information rather than requests for special treatment **Boundary-setting context:** Using disclosure to establish necessary limits or accommodations **Community building:** Sharing with others who might have similar experiences or understanding

Maria, a 30-year-old social worker, has developed her disclosure strategy: "I have different levels of explanation depending on the relationship and situation. For work events, I might just say I have sensory sensitivities and prefer quieter spaces. For close friends, I explain that I'm AuDHD and what specific support I need. For family, I've had detailed conversations about what autism and ADHD mean and how they can help me feel included rather than overwhelmed."

Exit strategies: Leaving events gracefully

Having clear exit strategies reduces social anxiety by ensuring you can leave overwhelming situations before reaching crisis points. This planning allows you to attempt social activities with less fear, knowing you have escape routes if needed.

Planning exit strategies in advance:

Transportation independence: Having your own vehicle or backup transportation options **Communication protocols:** Agreed-upon signals with your partner about readiness to leave **Timing expectations:** Setting realistic duration limits before events begin **Excuse preparation:** Having socially acceptable reasons ready for early departures **Recovery planning:** Knowing what you'll do after leaving to restore energy

Exit strategy execution:

Early warning recognition: Identifying signs that you're approaching overwhelm before crisis hits **Partner communication:** Using predetermined signals to indicate need for departure **Graceful departure:** Leaving politely without extensive explanations or apologies **Recovery initiation:** Beginning restoration activities immediately after leaving **Follow-up consideration:** Deciding if any communication with hosts is needed

Sample exit scripts:

Gentle departure: "Thank you so much for including us. We need to head home now, but we really enjoyed seeing everyone."

Health-based exit: "I'm starting to feel unwell and don't want to risk getting anyone sick. Thanks for a lovely evening."

Schedule-based exit: "We have an early morning tomorrow, so we need to call it a night. Great party!"

Sensory overwhelm exit: "The music is getting a bit loud for me, so we're going to head out. Thanks for having us!"

Emergency exit: "Something's come up that we need to handle at home. Sorry to leave early, but thank you for inviting us."

Creating AuDHD-friendly gatherings: Hosting on your terms

Hosting social events allows you to control environmental factors and create neurodivergent-friendly social experiences. This can be more sustainable than attending events in overwhelming environments while still maintaining social connections.

AuDHD-friendly hosting principles:

Environmental control: Managing lighting, sound, temperature, and sensory factors **Activity structure:** Providing organized activities that reduce social pressure **Guest management:** Limiting numbers and choosing compatible people **Timing consideration:** Scheduling events for your optimal energy times **Escape availability:** Maintaining private spaces for regulation if needed

Environmental modifications for neurodivergent hosting:

Lighting adjustments: Using warm, dim lighting instead of harsh overhead fluorescents **Sound management:** Controlling music volume and eliminating background noise **Seating arrangements:** Providing various seating options including quiet corners **Sensory accommodations:** Offering fidget tools, weighted blankets, or noise-canceling headphones **Space organization:** Creating clear areas for different activities and energy levels

AuDHD hosting activity ideas:

Structured social activities: Game nights, movie screenings, or guided discussions **Parallel socializing:** Activities where people can interact while engaged in other tasks **Educational gatherings:** Sharing special interests or learning new skills together **Sensory-friendly celebrations:** Parties with accommodations for sensory differences **Small group connections:** Intimate gatherings that reduce social performance pressure

David, a 32-year-old engineer, hosts regular neurodivergent-friendly gatherings: "We have monthly game nights specifically for our neurodivergent friends and their partners. I keep the lights dim, provide fidget toys, and have a quiet room available if anyone needs a break. We play cooperative board games instead of competitive ones to reduce stress. Everyone knows they can leave early without explanation. It's become our main way of maintaining friendships because it works with our neurological needs instead of against them."

Finding your people: Building neurodivergent community

Creating connections with other neurodivergent individuals and couples can provide understanding, support, and social experiences that don't require masking or extensive accommodation requests. This community building reduces isolation while providing models for successful neurodivergent relationships.

Benefits of neurodivergent community:

Reduced masking: Social situations where you can be authentic without explanation **Shared understanding:** Others who understand your experiences without extensive education **Accommodation normalization:** Social environments designed with neurodivergent needs in mind **Support exchange:** Mutual assistance during difficult times or transitions **Relationship modeling:** Seeing examples of successful neurodivergent partnerships

Finding neurodivergent community:

Online communities: Social media groups, forums, and virtual meetups for neurodivergent individuals **Local support groups:** In-person meetings for autism, ADHD, or general neurodivergent support **Special interest groups:** Communities organized around shared interests that attract neurodivergent people **Professional networks:** Workplace or career-focused neurodivergent professional groups **Advocacy organizations:** Groups focused on neurodivergent rights and awareness

Building relationships within neurodivergent community:

Gradual connection: Starting with low-pressure online interaction before meeting in person **Interest-based bonding:** Connecting through shared special interests or hobbies **Support exchange:** Offering help with others' challenges while receiving support for your own **Authentic communication:** Using direct, honest communication styles that feel natural **Accommodation collaboration:** Working together to create accessible social experiences

Couples-focused neurodivergent community building:

Partner inclusion: Finding communities that welcome and include both neurodivergent and neurotypical partners **Relationship support:** Connecting with other couples facing similar challenges **Social modeling:** Learning from successful neurodivergent relationships **Advocacy partnership:** Working together on neurodivergent awareness and acceptance **Resource sharing:** Exchanging information about therapists, strategies, and accommodations

Lisa, a 31-year-old nurse, found her community through online connections: "I started in an AuDHD Facebook group and eventually met several people locally. Now we have a core group of four couples who get together monthly. We understand each other's needs without explanation—everyone knows that parties have quiet spaces, gatherings have time limits, and people can leave early without offense. It's the first social group where I've felt completely comfortable being myself."

Practical Social Navigation Tools

Social Energy Assessment Tool

Evaluate social commitments before committing:

Event evaluation criteria:

- Duration of social obligation and energy requirements
- Sensory environment and accommodation possibilities
- Relationship importance and social benefit potential
- Current energy reserves and upcoming demands
- Recovery time available after social activity

Capacity assessment questions:

- What is my current social energy level on a 1-10 scale?
- How many social spoons do I have available this week?
- What other energy demands am I managing currently?

- How much recovery time will I need after this event?
- What support will I need during and after this social activity?

Decision-making framework:

- Does this event align with my relationship priorities?
- Can I participate authentically without extensive masking?
- Are appropriate accommodations available or requestable?
- Do I have adequate recovery time planned afterward?
- What is the cost-benefit ratio for my energy investment?

Event Survival Kit Checklist

Prepare for social situations with supportive tools:

Sensory regulation items:

- Noise-canceling headphones or earplugs
- Sunglasses for light sensitivity
- Fidget tools or stim toys
- Comfortable layers for temperature regulation

Communication aids:

- Prepared scripts for common social situations
- Business cards with contact information to avoid small talk
- Phone with trusted contacts for support check-ins
- Notes app for important information that might be forgotten

Comfort and recovery tools:

- Snacks for blood sugar maintenance
- Water bottle for hydration
- Medications or supplements as needed
- Transportation backup plans for early departure

Emergency regulation supplies:

- Hand sanitizer or wet wipes for sensory comfort
- Mints or gum for oral sensory needs
- Essential oils or preferred scents for grounding
- Emergency contact information for crisis support

Boundary Script Library for Social Situations

Practice responses for common social pressures:

For declining invitations: "That sounds fun, but it's not a good fit for my energy right now. Let's plan something smaller next week."

For requesting accommodations: "I'd love to come, but I'll need to step outside periodically due to sensory sensitivities. Is that okay?"

For explaining early departures: "We need to leave now to stick to our evening routine, but thank you for including us."

For managing unsolicited advice: "I appreciate your concern, but we've found approaches that work well for our needs."

For addressing persistent pressure: "I understand you want us to be more social, but we need to manage our activities based on our neurological needs."

Social Situation Quick Exits

Immediate exit strategies:

- "I'm not feeling well and need to step outside for some air"
- "I just remembered we have an important call we need to take"
- "Something urgent has come up at home that we need to handle"

Planned departure strategies:

- "We have an early morning and need to head home soon"
- "Thank you for having us. We're going to call it a night"

- "This has been lovely, but we need to stick to our schedule"

Recovery initiation:

- Leave immediately without extended goodbyes
- Go directly to quiet, comfortable environment
- Begin preferred regulation activities immediately
- Avoid analysis or processing until regulated

Balancing Connection and Protection

Social life as an AuDHD couple requires constant balancing between connection and protection, between maintaining relationships and preserving your energy, between appearing socially acceptable and honoring your authentic needs. This balance shifts based on your current capacity, life circumstances, and relationship priorities.

The goal isn't to become perfectly social or completely isolated—it's to create sustainable approaches to social connection that work with your neurology rather than against it. This includes both participating in broader social networks and building specific neurodivergent community that understands and accommodates your needs.

These social navigation skills support all other aspects of your AuDHD relationship by reducing external pressures, providing community support, and creating environments where you can practice authentic connection with understanding people.

Social Boundary Mastery

- Social energy is finite and must be budgeted carefully between different relationships and obligations
- Boundary setting with others protects couple time and individual capacity without requiring extensive justification
- Strategic disclosure helps others understand your needs while maintaining appropriate privacy boundaries
- Exit strategies reduce social anxiety by ensuring you can leave overwhelming situations before crisis points

- Neurodivergent community provides understanding and support that reduces isolation while honoring authentic needs

Chapter 13: When both partners are neurodivergent

The kitchen sink overflows while you both stand frozen in executive function paralysis. Your partner's ADHD makes them unable to initiate the cleanup task. Your autism makes the sensory chaos overwhelming. You both know exactly what needs to happen, but neither can take the first step. This isn't relationship dysfunction—this is Tuesday evening in a dual-neurodivergent household.

Research from Embrace Autism shows that relationships where both partners are neurodivergent create unique dynamics that don't exist in neurotypical-neurodivergent pairings. You share deep understanding of each other's neurological experiences, but you also face the challenge of supporting each other when you're both struggling with similar issues.

These relationships can be incredibly fulfilling because the level of mutual understanding runs deeper than most couples ever experience. But they also require specific strategies for times when both partners need support simultaneously, or when your shared challenges compound rather than complement each other.

The double-edged sword: Shared understanding vs. shared struggles

Dual-neurodivergent relationships offer profound understanding alongside unique challenges. Your partner truly gets why sudden schedule changes trigger anxiety, why certain textures feel unbearable, or why social events require three days of recovery. This understanding creates intimacy that many couples never achieve.

But shared neurological patterns also mean you might both struggle with the same issues simultaneously. Executive function challenges affect both partners. Sensory overwhelm hits you at the same time. Social energy depletion happens on similar schedules. Traditional relationship advice assumes one partner can compensate for the other's struggles, but that doesn't work when you're both facing identical challenges.

The benefits of shared neurodivergent understanding:

Authentic acceptance: No need to mask or explain basic neurological differences **Reduced judgment:** Understanding that challenging behaviors stem from neurology, not character **Accommodation normalization:** Environmental and lifestyle modifications feel natural rather than burdensome **Communication ease:** Direct, honest communication styles that both partners appreciate **Shared advocacy:** Working together for neurodivergent-friendly environments and understanding

The challenges of shared neurodivergent struggles:

Simultaneous overwhelm: Both partners hitting capacity limits at the same time **Compounding executive dysfunction:** Neither partner can initiate solutions when both are stuck **Mutual sensory triggers:** Environmental factors that overwhelm both people simultaneously **Parallel processing needs:** Both requiring alone time or space at the same moments **Support capacity limits:** Neither partner having bandwidth to provide care when both need it

Consider Sarah and Emma's experience as a dual-AuDHD couple in their late twenties: "The best thing about our relationship is that we never have to explain why we need things. Emma understands when I need to leave parties early. I understand when she gets hyperfocused and forgets to eat. But the hardest thing is when we're both struggling at once. Last month, we both hit burnout simultaneously and neither of us could handle basic household tasks. We lived on takeout for two weeks because grocery shopping felt impossible for both of us."

Their experience illustrates how shared understanding becomes both the greatest strength and biggest challenge in dual-neurodivergent relationships.

The support see-saw: Taking turns being the strong one

Successful dual-neurodivergent relationships develop systems for alternating support roles. Since both partners face similar neurological challenges, you need frameworks for taking turns being the stronger, more capable partner when the other is struggling.

Principles of support role alternation:

Recognize capacity fluctuations: Both partners' abilities vary daily based on energy, stress, and circumstances **Communicate current status:** Clear ways to express when you need support versus when you can provide it **Accept temporary imbalances:** Understanding that support roles won't always be perfectly equal **Plan for mutual struggles:** Protocols for times when both partners are simultaneously overwhelmed **Celebrate reciprocity:** Acknowledging and appreciating when support flows in both directions

Creating support trading systems:

Daily check-ins: Morning conversations about each partner's current capacity and support needs **Role clarification:** Clear communication about who's handling which responsibilities on any given day **Capacity signaling:** Simple ways to communicate current ability to give or need to receive support **Backup planning:** Strategies for when both partners are below capacity simultaneously **Recovery coordination:** Taking turns having periods of higher support needs

Take Marcus and David's approach as a neurodivergent couple: "We do daily capacity check-ins using a traffic light system. Green means I can handle my stuff and help with yours. Yellow means I can handle my responsibilities but can't take on extra. Red means I need active support with basic tasks. We've learned that it's okay for both of us to be yellow or even red sometimes—that's when we rely on our external support systems and just focus on survival mode until one of us can get back to green."

Support see-saw strategies:

Strength-based role assignment: The partner with higher current capacity takes on more demanding tasks **Temporary responsibility**

shifts: Flexible distribution of household and relationship maintenance based on current ability **Energy pooling:** Combining available resources when both partners have limited but non-zero capacity **External support activation:** Reaching out to friends, family, or professionals when both partners need help **Recovery protection:** The less overwhelmed partner protects the more struggling partner's recovery time

Parallel processing: When both need space simultaneously

Dual-neurodivergent couples often face situations where both partners need alone time, sensory breaks, or processing space at the same time. This creates logistical challenges in shared living spaces and relationship maintenance, but it's a completely normal occurrence that requires planning rather than panic.

Common parallel processing scenarios:

Post-social recovery: Both partners needing alone time after social events or challenging interactions **Sensory overwhelm:** Both experiencing environmental overstimulation that requires retreat to quiet spaces **Executive function shutdown:** Both partners feeling stuck and unable to handle decision-making or task initiation **Emotional processing:** Both needing time to work through feelings after conflicts or difficult conversations **Special interest hyperfocus:** Both partners deeply engaged in individual interests without social energy

Strategies for simultaneous space needs:

Space designation: Creating separate areas where each partner can retreat without disturbing the other **Time coordination:** Scheduling parallel processing time so both partners get needed space **Communication protocols:** Ways to signal space needs without lengthy explanations or negotiations **Reconnection planning:** Predetermined times for checking in and reengaging after parallel processing **External space utilization:** Using libraries, cafes, or outdoor spaces when home doesn't provide adequate separation

Creating parallel processing frameworks:

Physical space solutions:

- Separate bedrooms or retreat spaces for individual regulation
- Noise-canceling arrangements that allow simultaneous space use
- Outdoor or public spaces that provide individual retreat options
- Flexible furniture arrangements that can create temporary separation

Temporal space solutions:

- Alternating processing time when space is limited
- Scheduled alone time that both partners can count on
- Flexible timing based on current needs and capacity
- Emergency space protocols for unexpected overwhelm

Communication during parallel processing:

- Clear signals for "need space" versus "available for connection"
- Methods for requesting needs without extensive discussion
- Ways to offer care without disrupting processing
- Protocols for reconnecting after individual space time

Lisa and Jennifer developed their parallel processing system: "We both get sensory overload at similar times, especially evening when we're both depleted from work. Our apartment isn't big enough for us to both hide in separate rooms, so we created a time-sharing system. I get the bedroom from 6-7 PM for my regulation time, then Jennifer gets it from 7-8 PM. During the other person's time, the partner in the living room uses noise-canceling headphones and engages in quiet activities. At 8 PM, we check in about whether we're ready to connect or if we need more parallel time."

Strength combining: Leveraging different abilities

Even when both partners are neurodivergent, you typically have different strength patterns that can complement each other. Your autism might make you excellent at research and planning while your partner's ADHD makes them great at brainstorming and taking action. Learning to leverage these differences creates powerful partnership dynamics.

Identifying complementary neurodivergent strengths:

Autism strengths that can support ADHD challenges:

- Systematic planning and organization can help with ADHD executive function struggles
- Detailed research abilities can support ADHD impulsive decision-making
- Pattern recognition can help identify ADHD behavioral patterns and triggers
- Routine creation can provide structure that supports ADHD functioning

ADHD strengths that can support autism challenges:

- Flexibility and adaptability can help with autism's difficulty with unexpected changes
- Creative problem-solving can find novel solutions to autism's specific challenges
- High energy periods can motivate autism's task initiation difficulties
- Spontaneity can introduce beneficial novelty into autism's routine preferences

Cross-condition support strategies:

- The partner with better current executive function handles planning and organization
- The partner with higher social energy manages social obligations and communications
- The partner with more sensory tolerance handles challenging environmental tasks

- The partner with better emotional regulation provides support during dysregulated periods

Creating strength-mapping systems:

Individual assessment: Each partner identifies their current strengths and challenges **Dynamic evaluation:** Regular check-ins about how strengths and challenges fluctuate **Role flexibility:** Allowing support roles to shift based on changing circumstances **Appreciation practices:** Acknowledging and celebrating each other's contributions **Growth mindset:** Supporting each other's development of skills and capacities

Michael and Tom mapped their complementary strengths: "I'm great at making detailed plans and researching options, but I get paralyzed when it's time to actually start tasks. Tom is terrible at planning but once he gets started on something, he can hyperfocus and complete it efficiently. So I do all the research and planning for our projects, then hand them off to Tom with clear action steps. He gets the satisfaction of completion, and I get the security of knowing things will be done properly."

The stuck-stuck scenario: Emergency protocols for mutual overwhelm

Sometimes both partners experience simultaneous overwhelm, shutdown, or crisis that leaves neither person capable of providing support or handling basic life tasks. Having emergency protocols prevents these situations from becoming relationship disasters.

Warning signs of mutual overwhelm:

Both partners showing stress symptoms: Increased irritability, withdrawal, or emotional volatility **Household management breakdown:** Basic tasks like cleaning, cooking, or bill-paying falling behind **Communication deterioration:** Decreased ability to connect, share, or problem-solve together **External obligation struggles:** Missing appointments, social commitments, or work responsibilities

Self-care decline: Both partners neglecting basic health, hygiene, or wellness needs

Emergency protocol elements:

Immediate safety: Ensuring basic needs are met when both partners are incapacitated **External support activation:** Predetermined contacts who can provide practical assistance **Reduced expectations:** Temporarily lowering standards for household and relationship maintenance **Basic functioning focus:** Prioritizing only essential tasks until capacity returns **Recovery planning:** Structured approach to gradually rebuilding normal functioning

Practical emergency protocols:

24-hour survival mode:

- Focus only on basic needs like food, hydration, and safety
- Eliminate all non-essential responsibilities and obligations
- Use external resources like food delivery and household services
- Postpone all major decisions or challenging conversations

External support activation:

- Contact predetermined support people for practical assistance
- Reach out to professional help if needed for mental health support
- Utilize community resources like grocery delivery or household services
- Consider temporary separation if space would be helpful for recovery

Recovery initiation:

- Start with the partner who shows first signs of increased capacity
- Begin with smallest possible tasks to rebuild sense of capability

- Gradually increase responsibilities as both partners regain functioning
- Debrief the experience to improve future emergency protocols

Emergency Protocols for Dual Meltdowns

Immediate response:

- Both partners retreat to separate safe spaces if possible
- Focus on individual regulation before attempting to support each other
- Use pre-established comfort items or regulation tools
- Avoid attempting to communicate until both are regulated

Safety prioritization:

- Ensure physical safety of both partners and any dependents
- Remove or reduce environmental triggers if possible
- Contact emergency support person if situation seems dangerous
- Focus on basic needs like hydration and comfort

Recovery coordination:

- Check in briefly once initial crisis has passed
- Determine which partner can take minimal action if needed
- Plan simple, low-demand activities for immediate period
- Schedule follow-up processing once both partners are stable

Celebrating neurodivergent love: Unique joys and connections

Dual-neurodivergent relationships offer forms of intimacy and connection that are difficult to achieve in neurotypical relationships. The shared understanding, authentic communication, and mutual accommodation create unique joys worth celebrating.

Unique intimacies in neurodivergent relationships:

Authentic self-expression: Complete freedom to be yourself without masking or performance **Shared special interests:** Deep connection through mutual fascination with specific topics **Sensory compatibility:** Understanding and accommodating each other's sensory needs naturally **Communication honesty:** Direct, clear communication without hidden meanings or social games **Mutual advocacy:** Supporting each other's needs in the broader world

Special relationship dynamics:

Hyperfocus sharing: Engaging together in intense focus on shared interests or projects **Stimming together:** Comfortable self-regulation in each other's presence **Routine harmony:** Creating daily patterns that support both partners' neurological needs **Crisis understanding:** True comprehension of each other's overwhelm and shutdown experiences **Growth partnership:** Supporting each other's neurodivergent self-discovery and development

Celebrating your unique connection:

Acknowledge your depth: Recognize the level of understanding you share that most couples never achieve **Honor your authenticity:** Celebrate the freedom to be completely yourself in your relationship **Appreciate your resilience:** Acknowledge how you support each other through neurological challenges **Value your advocacy:** Recognize your partnership in creating neurodivergent-friendly environments **Embrace your differences:** Celebrate how your unique neurological combinations create something special

Rachel and Alex reflect on their dual-neurodivergent relationship: "People sometimes ask if it's harder being in a relationship where both partners have challenges. But we don't see our neurological differences as challenges—we see them as the foundation of our deepest connection. Alex understands why I need three hours of alone time after social events. I understand when they get hyperfocused on a project and forget to eat. We don't have to explain ourselves or apologize for our brains. We can just be authentic together in ways that feel impossible with neurotypical people."

Practical Tools for Dual-Neurodivergent Success

Support Role Trading System

Create clear frameworks for alternating support responsibilities:

Daily capacity check-in:

- Morning assessment of each partner's current capacity level
- Clear communication about energy, emotional state, and availability
- Identification of who needs more support versus who can provide it
- Flexible role assignment based on current circumstances

Support responsibility matrix:

- List of household and relationship tasks that can be shared
- Clear protocols for who handles what based on current capacity
- Backup plans for when neither partner can handle certain responsibilities
- Regular review and adjustment of responsibility distribution

Support quality assessment:

- Recognition of different types of support each partner can provide
- Matching support offered to support needed based on current circumstances
- Appreciation for support given even when it doesn't perfectly match what's needed
- Understanding that support capacity varies and that's normal

Mutual Overwhelm Action Plan

Prepare for times when both partners are struggling:

Prevention strategies:

- Regular monitoring of stress levels and early warning signs
- Proactive reduction of obligations when both partners show stress symptoms
- Environmental modifications to reduce overwhelm triggers
- Scheduling recovery time before crisis points are reached

Crisis response protocol:

- Immediate safety assessment and basic needs prioritization
- External support activation including friends, family, or professionals
- Reduction of all non-essential responsibilities and expectations
- Focus on individual regulation before attempting relationship support

Recovery planning:

- Gradual reintroduction of normal responsibilities as capacity returns
- Processing of the overwhelm experience to improve future responses
- Adjustment of ongoing routines and expectations based on lessons learned
- Celebration of resilience and mutual support during difficult times

Strength-Mapping for Partnership

Identify and leverage complementary abilities:

Individual strength inventory:

- Each partner identifies their current neurological strengths and challenges
- Assessment of how these strengths fluctuate based on circumstances

- Recognition of how individual strengths can support the partnership
- Understanding of when individual challenges need external support

Complementary pairing analysis:

- Identification of how each partner's strengths can support the other's challenges
- Development of systems for leveraging complementary abilities
- Creation of backup plans for when both partners struggle in the same areas
- Regular review and adjustment as strengths and challenges change

Partnership optimization:

- Task assignment based on current strengths rather than arbitrary division
- Mutual appreciation for different types of contributions to the relationship
- Support for each partner's growth and development of new capacities
- Celebration of how your unique combination creates something greater than individual abilities

Building Your Neurodivergent Partnership

Dual-neurodivergent relationships require specific strategies that differ from both neurotypical relationships and mixed neurotypical-neurodivergent partnerships. The key lies in leveraging your shared understanding while developing systems for mutual support that account for your similar challenges.

The goal isn't to eliminate the difficulties that come with both partners being neurodivergent—it's to create frameworks that work with your combined neurological realities rather than against them. This requires ongoing communication, flexible systems, and external support networks that understand your unique dynamics.

These dual-neurodivergent relationship skills become especially important when addressing trauma and healing, since both partners may have neurological factors that affect how they process difficult experiences and support each other's recovery.

Partnership Mastery Principles

- Dual-neurodivergent relationships offer profound understanding alongside unique challenges requiring specialized strategies
- Support role alternation allows partners to take turns being strong when both face similar neurological struggles
- Parallel processing needs require planning for simultaneous space and regulation requirements
- Complementary neurodivergent strengths can be leveraged to create powerful partnership dynamics
- Emergency protocols for mutual overwhelm prevent crisis situations from damaging relationship stability

Chapter 14: Trauma, healing, and moving forward

Your partner reaches out to touch your shoulder during a difficult conversation, and you suddenly feel like you can't breathe. The touch was gentle and loving, but your nervous system reacts as though you're in danger. Is this autism sensory sensitivity, ADHD emotional dysregulation, trauma response, or all three at once? Sorting out these overlapping experiences becomes essential for healing within your relationship.

Research shows that neurodivergent individuals experience trauma at significantly higher rates than neurotypical populations, often starting in childhood with experiences of rejection, bullying, or systemic discrimination for being different. The intersection of trauma with AuDHD traits creates complex presentations that require careful untangling.

Your healing journey doesn't happen in isolation—it occurs within the context of your relationship, where your partner's responses can either support or hinder your recovery. Learning to distinguish trauma responses from neurological traits while building safety together becomes the foundation for post-traumatic growth.

The trauma-AuDHD tangle: Sorting out what's what

Trauma responses and AuDHD traits often look similar, making it difficult to determine what needs healing versus what needs accommodation. A startle response to unexpected touch could be autism sensory sensitivity, trauma-related hypervigilance, or both. Social withdrawal might stem from ADHD rejection sensitivity, trauma-based trust issues, or autism social exhaustion.

Overlapping presentations of trauma and AuDHD:

Hypervigilance vs. sensory sensitivity: Both create heightened awareness of environmental stimuli **Social withdrawal vs.**

introversion: Both involve avoiding or limiting social interaction **Emotional dysregulation vs. ADHD intensity:** Both create strong emotional responses that feel overwhelming **Control needs vs. autism routines:** Both involve desire for predictability and environmental management **Memory issues vs. ADHD working memory:** Both affect ability to remember events clearly

Key differences between trauma responses and AuDHD traits:

Trauma responses typically:

- Developed after specific harmful experiences
- Create fear-based reactions to stimuli
- Involve avoidance of reminders of traumatic events
- Include intrusive thoughts or flashbacks
- Cause disconnection from your own body and emotions

AuDHD traits typically:

- Present consistently throughout your life
- Represent neurological differences in processing
- Create preferences rather than fears
- Are manageable with appropriate accommodations
- Feel like authentic parts of your identity

The importance of accurate sorting:

Understanding which experiences stem from trauma versus neurology determines appropriate interventions. Trauma responses need healing approaches that address the underlying wounds. AuDHD traits need acceptance and accommodation rather than attempts to eliminate them.

Consider Jennifer's experience sorting her responses: "I used to think my need for routine and predictability was all trauma-related because my childhood was chaotic and unsafe. But when I started learning about autism, I realized that some of my structure needs are neurological. The trauma made me hypervigilant about changes, but my autism brain actually functions better with routine. Now I can work on healing the trauma-fear around change while still honoring my neurological need for structure."

Jennifer's process illustrates how trauma and neurology can interact without being identical. Her trauma intensified existing neurological traits, but addressing the trauma didn't eliminate her authentic neurological needs.

Window of tolerance: Why yours is different

The window of tolerance—your capacity to handle stress and emotional activation without becoming overwhelmed—operates differently for AuDHD individuals. Research from Betterfamilytherapy shows that neurodivergent nervous systems typically have narrower windows of tolerance, meaning you reach overwhelm more quickly than neurotypical individuals.

Factors affecting AuDHD window of tolerance:

Sensory processing differences: Environmental stimuli that don't affect others can push you outside your window **Executive function demands:** Mental tasks that seem simple to others can be overwhelming for your brain **Social interaction costs:** Communication and relationship maintenance require more energy, reducing your capacity **Masking exhaustion:** Suppressing authentic self-expression depletes resources needed for emotional regulation **Rejection sensitivity:** Fear of criticism or abandonment creates chronic low-level activation

How trauma affects your window of tolerance:

Narrowed capacity: Trauma typically reduces your ability to handle stress without becoming overwhelmed **Trigger sensitivity:** Specific reminders of traumatic experiences instantly push you outside your window **Hyperarousal patterns:** Tendency to become activated more quickly and intensely than pre-trauma **Hypoarousal patterns:** Tendency to shut down or disconnect when overwhelmed **Recovery**

difficulties: Longer time needed to return to baseline functioning after activation

Expanding your window of tolerance:

Nervous system regulation: Practices that help you stay within your optimal functioning zone **Trigger identification:** Understanding what pushes you outside your window so you can prepare or avoid **Early intervention:** Recognizing activation before it becomes overwhelming and taking action **Recovery skills:** Techniques for returning to your window when you've been pushed outside it **Environmental modifications:** Reducing stimuli that unnecessarily stress your nervous system

Window of tolerance in relationships:

Your partner's understanding of your window of tolerance dramatically affects your healing and relationship quality. When they recognize your capacity limits and support your regulation efforts, you can gradually expand your window. When they push you beyond your limits or dismiss your needs, your window often becomes even narrower.

Take Michael's experience with his partner learning about his window of tolerance: "My boyfriend used to think I was being dramatic when I said I needed to leave parties after an hour. He'd push me to stay longer, saying everyone was having fun. But when I explained that my window of tolerance is smaller than his and that staying longer would push me into overwhelm that would affect our relationship for days, he started supporting my need to leave early. Now I can actually enjoy the parts of social events that fit within my window because I'm not constantly worried about being pushed beyond my limits."

Healing in connection: Trauma recovery in relationships

Traditional trauma therapy often focuses on individual healing, but relationship trauma—which is common for neurodivergent individuals—requires healing within the context of safe relationships.

Your partner can become a co-regulator who helps expand your window of tolerance and provides corrective experiences of safety.

Principles of trauma healing in relationships:

Safety first: Physical and emotional safety must be established before trauma processing can begin **Paced processing:** Trauma work proceeds at the survivor's pace, not according to external timelines **Choice and control:** Healing requires autonomy over the process, timing, and depth of exploration **Co-regulation:** Partners can help stabilize the nervous system during difficult moments **Corrective experiences:** New relationship experiences that contradict trauma-based beliefs

How partners can support trauma healing:

Consistent safety: Reliable, predictable behavior that builds trust over time **Emotional attunement:** Recognizing and responding appropriately to emotional needs **Respect for autonomy:** Honoring the survivor's choices about healing process and pace **Education and understanding:** Learning about trauma and its effects to provide informed support **Patience with healing:** Understanding that recovery is nonlinear and takes significant time

Challenges in relationship-based trauma healing:

Triggered reactions: Trauma responses can be activated by loving partners who remind you of past harm **Projection risks:** Transferring expectations from past relationships onto current partner **Healing pace differences:** Partners may heal at different rates or have different trauma histories **Support capacity limits:** Partners may not always have bandwidth to provide needed support **Professional support needs:** Some trauma healing requires specialized professional intervention

Creating healing environments in relationships:

Predictable safety: Consistent daily routines and interactions that build nervous system stability **Clear communication:** Direct, honest conversation about needs, triggers, and boundaries **Flexible support:** Adjusting support approaches based on current healing needs and capacity **Growth celebration:** Acknowledging progress and resilience throughout the healing journey **Professional integration:** Combining relationship support with appropriate professional trauma treatment

Sarah describes healing trauma within her relationship: "I was sexually assaulted in college, and physical intimacy in relationships became terrifying. My girlfriend and I worked together to rebuild my sense of safety around touch. We started with holding hands while fully clothed and worked up to more intimate contact over months. She never pushed my boundaries and always checked in about my comfort level. Having someone respect my healing pace and support my recovery made it possible to heal in ways I couldn't do alone."

Safety first protocols: Building trust gradually

Trust-building after trauma requires concrete actions rather than just good intentions. AuDHD individuals often need explicit evidence of safety because your pattern recognition abilities allow you to notice inconsistencies that might signal danger.

Elements of trauma-informed safety building:

Behavioral consistency: Actions matching words over extended periods **Boundary respect:** Immediate, consistent honoring of stated limits and preferences **Emotional regulation:** Partner's ability to manage their own emotions without making you responsible **Transparent communication:** Clear, honest information about intentions, feelings, and plans **Patience with healing:** Understanding that trust rebuilds slowly and setbacks are normal

Practical safety-building strategies:

Start small: Begin with low-risk trust situations and gradually increase vulnerability **Communicate explicitly:** State your needs and boundaries clearly rather than expecting intuition **Document**

patterns: Track evidence of trustworthiness to counteract trauma-based hypervigilance **Practice repair:** Work through inevitable misunderstandings and mistakes with compassion **Seek support:** Utilize professional help when needed to support the trust-building process

Safety protocols for specific trauma types:

For physical trauma: Clear consent protocols, respect for physical boundaries, predictable physical interactions **For emotional trauma:** Validation of feelings, emotional safety during conflicts, consistent emotional availability **For sexual trauma:** Explicit consent processes, respect for sexual boundaries, patient rebuilding of physical intimacy **For attachment trauma:** Consistent availability, reliable follow-through on commitments, patience with trust-building

Red flags that indicate safety is not present:

Boundary violations: Pushing past stated limits or minimizing the importance of boundaries **Gaslighting:** Making you question your memories, perceptions, or reactions **Emotional volatility:** Unpredictable emotional reactions that create fear or hypervigilance **Manipulation:** Using guilt, threats, or coercion to get needs met **Dismissiveness:** Minimizing trauma history or its impact on current functioning

Lisa worked with her partner to establish safety after childhood trauma: "My dad was emotionally abusive, so I'm hypervigilant about anger and criticism. My partner and I created specific protocols for disagreements—we speak in calm voices, take breaks if emotions get intense, and always reassure each other about the relationship after conflicts. It took two years of consistent behavior before I could believe these protocols would actually be followed, but now I feel genuinely safe during conflicts for the first time in my life."

When therapy helps: Finding neurodivergent-affirming support

Professional trauma therapy can significantly support healing when therapists understand both trauma and neurodivergence. Research from PubMed Central shows that neurodivergent-affirming therapy approaches lead to better outcomes for autistic and ADHD individuals.

Characteristics of neurodivergent-affirming trauma therapy:

Neurodivergent positive: Views autism and ADHD as neurological differences rather than disorders to cure **Sensory aware:** Understands how sensory processing affects therapy process and healing **Communication flexible:** Adapts therapeutic approaches to match neurodivergent communication styles **Pace responsive:** Adjusts therapy timing and intensity based on neurodivergent processing needs **Strength focused:** Builds on neurodivergent strengths rather than focusing only on challenges

Types of therapy approaches helpful for AuDHD trauma healing:

EMDR (Eye Movement Desensitization and Reprocessing): Effective for processing traumatic memories with minimal verbal processing required **Somatic therapy:** Focuses on body-based healing that addresses trauma stored in the nervous system **DBT (Dialectical Behavior Therapy):** Teaches emotional regulation skills particularly helpful for rejection sensitivity **IFS (Internal Family Systems):** Helps integrate different parts of self including neurological traits **Trauma-informed CBT:** Cognitive approaches adapted for trauma recovery and neurodivergent thinking patterns

Finding the right trauma therapist:

Dual competency: Expertise in both trauma treatment and neurodivergent populations **Therapeutic alliance:** Feeling understood and respected in the therapeutic relationship **Approach flexibility:** Willingness to adapt methods based on your specific needs and responses **Collaborative stance:** Including you as an expert on your own experience and healing needs **Professional development:** Ongoing education about neurodivergent-affirming practices

Integrating therapy with relationship healing:

Partner education: Therapists can help partners understand trauma and how to provide appropriate support **Couples sessions:** Joint sessions focused on healing within the relationship context **Communication skills:** Learning to communicate about trauma needs and triggers effectively **Support coordination:** Ensuring therapy work and relationship support complement rather than conflict **Progress integration:** Applying therapy insights and skills within the relationship context

David found neurodivergent-affirming trauma therapy: "I tried three different therapists before finding one who understood both autism and trauma. The first two wanted to 'fix' my social difficulties and saw my need for routine as trauma symptoms to eliminate. My current therapist helps me heal trauma while honoring my neurological differences. She understands that my social exhaustion is autism, not trauma, but my fear of criticism comes from childhood bullying that needs healing."

Post-traumatic growth: Building resilience together

Post-traumatic growth refers to positive changes that can emerge from trauma recovery—increased self-awareness, deeper relationships, stronger personal values, and greater appreciation for life. For AuDHD individuals, this growth often includes better understanding and acceptance of neurological differences.

Areas of post-traumatic growth in AuDHD individuals:

Self-understanding: Deeper knowledge of your neurological traits, needs, and strengths **Relationship capacity:** Ability to form deeper, more authentic connections with understanding partners **Advocacy skills:** Confidence in communicating your needs and educating others about neurodivergence **Resilience building:** Stronger coping skills for handling future challenges and setbacks **Life purpose:** Clearer sense of values and goals that align with your authentic self

Supporting post-traumatic growth in relationships:

Celebrate progress: Acknowledging and appreciating healing milestones and growth achievements **Support identity integration:** Helping each other integrate trauma recovery with neurodivergent identity **Encourage advocacy:** Supporting each other's efforts to communicate needs and educate others **Build meaning:** Finding purpose and significance in your healing journey and relationship growth **Share wisdom:** Using your experiences to help other neurodivergent individuals and couples

Growth-oriented healing practices:

Narrative therapy: Telling your story in ways that highlight resilience and growth rather than only trauma **Strength identification:** Recognizing abilities and resources developed through healing process **Value clarification:** Understanding what matters most based on your healing and growth experiences **Future visioning:** Creating hopeful goals and dreams that incorporate your healed and authentic self **Community building:** Connecting with others who share similar healing and growth experiences

Rachel reflects on her post-traumatic growth: "Healing from childhood bullying helped me understand that my autism isn't something to hide or be ashamed of. I went from trying to appear neurotypical to advocating for neurodivergent students in my school district. My relationship with my husband became deeper because I stopped masking and could be authentic. The trauma was horrible, but healing from it led me to a life that actually fits who I am."

Practical Trauma Healing Tools

Trauma vs. Trait Sorting Exercise

Systematically separate trauma responses from neurological traits:

Response evaluation criteria:

- When did this response pattern first appear in your life?
- Does this response involve fear or anxiety versus preference?
- Can this be accommodated versus does it need healing?
- Does this feel like an authentic part of you versus something imposed by harmful experiences?

Trauma response indicators:

- Developed after specific harmful experiences
- Involves fear-based avoidance or hypervigilance
- Creates disconnection from your authentic self
- Interferes with relationships or life functioning
- Improves with trauma-specific healing approaches

Neurological trait indicators:

- Present consistently throughout your life
- Involves preferences or processing differences
- Feels like an authentic part of your identity
- Manageable with appropriate accommodations
- Stable across different life circumstances

Safety Building Checklist

Track evidence of safety in your relationship:

Behavioral consistency tracking:

- Partner follows through on commitments and promises
- Actions match stated intentions over time
- Responses remain stable during stress or conflict
- Boundaries are respected immediately and consistently

Emotional safety indicators:

- You feel heard and validated during emotional conversations
- Partner takes responsibility for their own emotional regulation
- Conflicts are handled with respect and care
- Emotional needs are treated as valid and important

Physical safety evidence:

- All physical boundaries are respected without question
- Physical interactions feel comfortable and consensual
- Partner supports your sensory and physical needs
- You feel physically safe and protected in their presence

Healing Milestone Tracker

Document progress in trauma recovery:

Capacity expansions:

- Increased ability to handle previously triggering situations
- Expanded window of tolerance for stress and emotion
- Growing comfort with vulnerability and intimacy
- Enhanced capacity for trust and connection

Skill development:

- Improved emotional regulation abilities
- Better communication about trauma needs and triggers
- Stronger boundaries and self-advocacy skills
- Enhanced ability to distinguish past from present

Relationship improvements:

- Deeper intimacy and authentic connection with partner
- Reduced trauma reactions within the relationship
- Improved conflict resolution and repair abilities
- Greater capacity for giving and receiving support

Grounding Techniques for Couples

Immediate grounding for trauma activation:

- Partner sits nearby without touching unless requested
- Counting or breathing exercises done together

- Naming objects in the room or other concrete observations
- Using preferred sensory comfort items or tools

Co-regulation strategies:

- Partner models calm breathing and voice tone
- Offering physical comfort if welcomed and helpful
- Engaging in simple, concrete activities together
- Using predetermined soothing activities or rituals

Recovery support:

- Gentle check-ins about safety and needs
- Offering practical support without taking over
- Respecting need for space versus need for connection
- Following up after activation has passed

Building Your Healing Partnership

Trauma healing within AuDHD relationships requires understanding the complex interactions between trauma responses and neurological traits, building safety through consistent actions rather than just words, and supporting each other's growth while seeking appropriate professional help when needed.

The goal isn't to eliminate all trauma responses or pretend they don't affect your relationship—it's to create an environment where healing can occur while both partners' neurological needs are honored and supported. This foundation of safety and understanding becomes especially important as you navigate major life changes and transitions together.

The skills you develop in trauma healing—communication, boundary setting, emotional regulation, and mutual support—directly support your ability to handle life transitions and changes as a team.

Healing Journey Foundations

- Trauma responses and AuDHD traits often overlap but require different interventions for effective healing
- Narrower windows of tolerance in neurodivergent individuals require specialized approaches to safety and regulation
- Relationship-based healing provides corrective experiences while requiring consistent safety behaviors
- Neurodivergent-affirming trauma therapy addresses both healing needs and neurological differences
- Post-traumatic growth includes deeper self-understanding and stronger capacity for authentic relationships

Chapter 15: Growing through life transitions

The job offer arrives on a Tuesday, requiring a cross-country move within six weeks. Your autism brain immediately begins catastrophizing about routine disruption, new environments, and social adjustments. Your ADHD brain bounces between excitement about novelty and terror about the logistics. Meanwhile, your partner is asking about your feelings when you're still trying to process that this is actually happening.

Life transitions hit AuDHD individuals differently than neurotypical people. Your need for routine and predictability conflicts with change, while your executive function challenges make transition logistics overwhelming. Yet these same transitions often bring growth, opportunities, and positive changes that enhance your life and relationship.

Learning to navigate transitions together—both expected changes like career moves and unexpected crises like family emergencies—becomes a crucial skill for long-term relationship success. The strategies you develop can turn potentially overwhelming changes into manageable growth experiences.

Change through the AuDHD lens: Why transitions hit harder

Transitions challenge multiple aspects of AuDHD functioning simultaneously. Your autism brain loses familiar routines and predictable environments that provide security. Your ADHD brain faces executive function demands for planning and organization during emotionally challenging times. The combination creates perfect storm conditions for overwhelm.

Why transitions are particularly challenging for AuDHD:

Routine disruption: Changes to familiar patterns that provide emotional and sensory regulation **Sensory uncertainty:** Unknown environmental factors that might cause overwhelming stimulation **Executive function overload:** Complex planning and decision-making required during emotional stress **Social adjustments:** New people, places, and social expectations that require energy and adaptation **Uncertainty tolerance:** Difficulty managing ambiguous situations with unclear timelines or outcomes

How autism affects transition experiences:

Change resistance: Strong preference for familiar routines and environments **Sensory concerns:** Anxiety about unknown sensory environments and overwhelming stimulation **Social challenges:** Difficulty forming new relationships and understanding new social environments **Detail overwhelm:** Becoming stuck on specific aspects rather than seeing overall transition picture **Processing time needs:** Requiring more time to mentally adjust to change concepts

How ADHD affects transition experiences:

Executive function demands: Difficulty with planning, organizing, and managing complex transition logistics **Emotional dysregulation:** Intense feelings that interfere with logical decision-making and planning **Time management issues:** Difficulty estimating timelines and managing multiple transition tasks **Attention difficulties:** Trouble focusing on important details while managing transition stress **Impulsivity risks:** Making hasty decisions due to desire to resolve uncertainty quickly

Consider Maria's experience with a major career transition: "When I got accepted to graduate school, I spent three weeks in complete overwhelm. My autism brain kept listing all the things that would change—new city, new routines, new people, new environment. My ADHD brain couldn't organize all the logistics of moving, applying for loans, and coordinating timing. I would start research on apartments and get hyperfocused on comparing rental prices instead of actually applying anywhere. My boyfriend had to help me break everything into tiny, manageable steps before I could function."

Predictable passages: Moving, job changes, family additions

Some life transitions are predictable and can be planned for in advance. Recognizing these common passages and developing frameworks for handling them reduces stress and increases your capacity to navigate changes successfully.

Common predictable transitions for couples:

Geographic moves: Relocating for work, family, or lifestyle changes **Career changes:** Job transitions, education pursuits, or career direction shifts **Relationship evolution:** Moving in together, marriage, or other commitment changes **Family additions:** Having children, adopting pets, or welcoming aging relatives **Life stage transitions:** Graduating, retiring, or entering new phases of life

Frameworks for planned transitions:

Extended timeline planning: Beginning preparation months before actual transition occurs **Gradual adjustment strategies:** Making changes incrementally rather than all at once **Stress management protocols:** Building in extra support and reduced expectations during transition periods **Support system activation:** Engaging friends, family, and professionals to help with transition logistics **Recovery planning:** Scheduling post-transition recovery time for adjustment and emotional processing

Moving transition strategies:

Multiple visits: Traveling to new location several times before moving to build familiarity **Gradual packing:** Starting months early to avoid last-minute overwhelm **Routine recreation:** Identifying how to maintain important routines in new environment **Support network mapping:** Researching community resources and potential social connections **Sensory preparation:** Learning about climate, noise levels, and environmental factors

Career transition approaches:

Overlap periods: Maintaining current job while gradually transitioning to new role **Skill building:** Developing needed competencies before making career changes **Network development:** Building professional relationships in new field or location **Financial preparation:** Saving money to reduce financial stress during transition **Identity adjustment:** Processing changes to professional identity and daily routine

Lisa and her partner navigated a major career transition: "When I decided to leave teaching to become a therapist, we planned the transition over two years. I started graduate school part-time while still teaching, saved money to cover reduced income during internships, and gradually built my therapy skills through volunteer work. My husband took on more household responsibilities during my school years. By the time I left teaching, the transition felt manageable because we'd been preparing for so long."

The preparation protocol: Getting ready for known changes

AuDHD brains benefit from extensive preparation for known transitions. The more you can plan and prepare, the less overwhelming the actual change becomes. This preparation includes practical logistics, emotional adjustment, and system modifications.

Components of effective transition preparation:

Information gathering: Learning everything possible about upcoming changes and requirements **Skill development:** Building competencies needed for successful transition management **System creation:** Developing tools and frameworks for managing transition logistics **Support mobilization:** Activating help from partners, friends, family, and professionals **Stress management:** Building extra capacity for handling transition-related overwhelm

The six-month preparation timeline:

Months 6-4 before transition:

- Begin research and information gathering
- Start skill building and competency development
- Begin financial or practical preparation
- Discuss transition impact with partner and support network

Months 4-2 before transition:

- Finalize major decisions and logistics
- Create detailed transition plans and timelines
- Begin gradual adjustments where possible
- Increase support system involvement

Months 2-0 before transition:

- Execute detailed preparation plans
- Focus on stress management and emotional preparation
- Confirm all logistics and support arrangements
- Prepare for post-transition adjustment period

Emotional preparation strategies:

Visualization exercises: Mentally rehearsing successful transition outcomes **Grief processing:** Acknowledging losses involved in leaving familiar situations **Excitement cultivation:** Focusing on positive aspects and opportunities in upcoming changes **Fear addressing:** Identifying specific concerns and developing management strategies **Identity integration:** Understanding how change will affect your sense of self

Practical preparation tools:

Detailed checklists: Breaking down all transition tasks into manageable action items **Timeline management:** Creating realistic schedules that account for AuDHD processing needs **Resource compilation:** Gathering all needed information, contacts, and support resources **Backup planning:** Developing contingency plans for when primary approaches don't work **Progress tracking:** Monitoring preparation progress to maintain motivation and adjust timing

Michael prepared for relocating across the country: "We spent eight months preparing for our move. I visited our new city three times to scout neighborhoods and visit potential apartments. I researched autism support groups, ADHD-friendly doctors, and local community resources. We created a 47-item moving checklist and started working through it six months early. By moving day, I felt prepared instead of panicked because we'd addressed every detail I could think of."

Crisis navigation: When life throws curveballs

Unexpected changes—family emergencies, job loss, health crises, or relationship disruptions—require different strategies than planned transitions. These situations demand immediate response while your normal coping systems are disrupted by crisis stress.

Common types of unexpected transitions:

Health crises: Sudden illness, injury, or mental health challenges affecting you, your partner, or family members **Employment disruptions:** Unexpected job loss, workplace conflicts, or economic changes **Family emergencies:** Death, divorce, or crisis situations involving family members **Relationship disruptions:** Breakups, betrayals, or major conflicts that threaten relationship stability **Environmental crises:** Natural disasters, housing issues, or community disruptions

Crisis response framework for AuDHD:

Immediate stabilization: Focus on basic safety and essential needs before addressing complex decisions **Information gathering:** Collect only necessary information to avoid overwhelm from too much detail **Support activation:** Reach out to predetermined support network for practical and emotional help **Decision simplification:** Make only essential decisions and postpone non-urgent choices **Recovery**

planning: Build in rest and processing time between crisis management activities

Crisis communication strategies:

Clear information requests: Ask for specific, concrete information rather than general updates **Processing time acknowledgment:** Communicate that you need time to understand and respond to crisis information **Support specification:** Tell others exactly what type of help you need rather than accepting generic offers **Boundary maintenance:** Protect your capacity by limiting crisis-related communications and demands **Progress updates:** Keep key support people informed about your status and needs

Partner support during unexpected transitions:

Logistics management: Taking over practical tasks that might overwhelm the AuDHD partner **Information filtering:** Processing crisis information and presenting it in manageable chunks **Emotional regulation support:** Providing comfort and stability during overwhelming emotional reactions **Decision support:** Helping evaluate options and make decisions without taking over autonomy **Recovery protection:** Ensuring adequate rest and processing time during crisis management

Sarah navigated a family crisis when her father was hospitalized unexpectedly: "My autism brain wanted detailed medical information about his condition, but getting that information required phone calls that triggered my phone anxiety. My ADHD brain kept catastrophizing about worst-case scenarios. My girlfriend became my crisis coordinator—she made the phone calls, filtered information to give me what I needed without overwhelming details, and handled travel logistics for visiting him. I could focus on emotional processing and being present with my family instead of drowning in crisis management tasks."

Maintaining us: Couple connection during transitions

Transitions can strain relationships as both partners navigate stress, uncertainty, and changing circumstances. Maintaining connection requires intentional effort and modified expectations during transition periods.

How transitions affect couple dynamics:

Stress amplification: Individual stress affects both partners and relationship interactions **Role adjustments:** Changes in responsibilities and support needs during transition periods
Communication challenges: Increased emotional activation affecting ability to communicate clearly **Intimacy impacts:** Reduced capacity for physical and emotional intimacy during high-stress periods
Future focus conflicts: Different perspectives on transition outcomes and timeline preferences

Connection maintenance strategies:

Regular check-ins: Brief daily conversations about emotional state and current needs **Modified expectations:** Temporarily reducing relationship demands during high-stress transition periods **Stress sharing:** Distributing transition-related tasks based on current capacity and strengths **Comfort rituals:** Maintaining simple connection activities even when elaborate date nights aren't possible **Professional support:** Utilizing couples therapy or coaching during particularly challenging transitions

Transition-specific couple protocols:

Decision-making agreements: Clear processes for making transition-related decisions together **Support role clarification:** Understanding when each partner needs support versus when they can provide it **Communication modifications:** Adjusting conversation styles to account for transition stress **Intimacy adaptations:** Finding ways to maintain physical and emotional connection despite stress **Recovery coordination:** Planning post-transition time for relationship reconnection and processing

Preventing transition-related relationship damage:

Avoid major relationship decisions: Postponing significant relationship changes during transition stress **Maintain baseline connection:** Continuing minimum relationship maintenance activities **Address transition stress:** Acknowledging how change affects your relationship dynamics **Seek external support:** Getting help with transition logistics to preserve relationship energy **Plan reconnection:** Scheduling relationship-focused time after transition stress decreases

David and his partner maintained connection during graduate school: "The two years I was in school put huge stress on our relationship. We were both working and I was also taking classes, so we had almost no time together. We created a fifteen-minute morning connection ritual where we shared one thing we were looking forward to and one thing we needed support with. Even when everything else was chaotic, those fifteen minutes kept us connected. We also scheduled one three-hour block every other weekend for relationship time, even if it meant saying no to other opportunities."

Growth opportunities: Using change for relationship evolution

Transitions, while challenging, often provide opportunities for relationship growth, deeper intimacy, and positive changes that wouldn't occur during stable periods. Learning to identify and leverage these growth opportunities helps couples emerge stronger from difficult transitions.

Growth opportunities within transitions:

Increased intimacy: Supporting each other through vulnerability creates deeper emotional bonds **Skill development:** Learning new capacities for communication, problem-solving, and mutual support **Value clarification:** Understanding what matters most when external circumstances change **Resilience building:** Developing confidence in your ability to handle future challenges together **Authenticity expansion:** Reducing masks and pretenses when survival becomes more important than performance

Using transitions for positive relationship changes:

Communication improvements: Learning to express needs and provide support more effectively **Role renegotiation:** Adjusting responsibilities and expectations based on changing circumstances **Boundary refinement:** Clarifying what you need from each other and external relationships **Goal realignment:** Adjusting life goals and priorities based on transition experiences **Connection deepening:** Finding new ways to support and understand each other

Post-transition integration:

Experience processing: Discussing what you learned about yourselves and your relationship **System adjustment:** Modifying daily routines and relationship patterns based on transition insights **Growth celebration:** Acknowledging increased resilience, skills, and intimacy **Future preparation:** Using transition experience to prepare for next challenges **Wisdom sharing:** Helping other couples navigate similar transitions

Rachel reflects on growth through transitions: "Moving across the country for my husband's job was terrifying initially. But going through that transition together taught us how to support each other under pressure. I learned that he's incredibly practical and organized during crisis, which helps my ADHD brain stay focused. He learned that I need processing time but then become very decisive and action-oriented. We came out of that move knowing we could handle anything together."

Practical Transition Navigation Tools

Transition Preparation Checklist

Systematic approach to preparing for planned changes:

Information and research phase:

- Gather all available information about upcoming transition

- Research resources and support systems in new situation
- Identify potential challenges and obstacles to address
- Learn about timelines and requirements for successful transition

Skill and capacity building:

- Identify competencies needed for successful transition management
- Begin developing needed skills well before transition occurs
- Build financial or practical resources required for change
- Strengthen support networks and relationships

Logistics and planning:

- Create detailed timelines and task lists for transition management
- Develop contingency plans for potential complications
- Arrange practical support for transition logistics
- Prepare emotional and stress management strategies

Change Impact Assessment Tool

Evaluate how transitions will affect different life areas:

Routine and structure impact:

- Which daily routines will change and how to adapt them
- What environmental factors will be different and how to prepare
- How to maintain essential structure during transition period
- Timeline for establishing new routines in post-transition life

Relationship and social impact:

- How transition will affect your relationship dynamics
- What social connections might change and how to maintain important ones

- New social opportunities and challenges in post-transition situation
- Support network availability during and after transition

Sensory and environmental impact:

- New sensory environments and potential challenges
- How to modify new environments for optimal functioning
- What sensory supports to bring or establish in new situation
- Environmental factors that might require accommodation

Connection Maintenance Plan Template

Preserve relationship bond during transition stress:

Daily connection rituals:

- Brief check-ins about emotional state and immediate needs
- Simple affection or appreciation expressions
- Shared meals or activities when possible despite busy schedules
- Bedtime or morning connection routines

Weekly relationship maintenance:

- Longer conversations about transition progress and challenges
- Shared activities that provide stress relief and enjoyment
- Physical intimacy adapted to current energy and stress levels
- Planning and decision-making for transition logistics

Monthly relationship assessment:

- Discussion of how transition is affecting relationship dynamics
- Adjustment of expectations and support strategies as needed
- Celebration of progress and mutual support achievements
- Professional support consultation if relationship strain is significant

Transition Survival Quick Tips

For planning overwhelm:

- Break large transitions into smallest possible steps
- Focus on only the next immediate action required
- Use external support for logistics management when possible
- Set realistic timelines that account for AuDHD processing needs

For emotional overwhelm:

- Practice grounding techniques regularly during transition stress
- Maintain baseline self-care routines even when busy
- Communicate emotional needs clearly to partner and support network
- Consider professional support if emotional overwhelm becomes unmanageable

For relationship strain:

- Lower expectations for relationship perfection during transition periods
- Focus on essential connection activities and postpone optional relationship work
- Seek external support for practical tasks to preserve relationship energy
- Schedule relationship reconnection time for post-transition period

Thriving Through Change Together

Life transitions are inevitable parts of long-term relationships, and AuDHD individuals can learn to navigate them successfully with appropriate preparation, support, and strategies. The goal isn't to eliminate transition stress—it's to develop systems that help you handle change while maintaining your relationship connection and individual well-being.

The skills you develop in transition navigation—communication under pressure, mutual support during stress, and flexible problem-solving—strengthen your relationship's resilience for handling whatever life brings next. These experiences often reveal hidden strengths and capacities that increase confidence for future challenges.

Your journey through transitions as an AuDHD couple builds a foundation of trust, competence, and connection that supports all other aspects of your relationship. Each successfully navigated change increases your confidence that you can handle whatever comes next, together.

Transition Navigation Mastery

- AuDHD individuals experience transitions more intensely due to routine disruption and executive function demands
- Planned transitions benefit from extended preparation timelines and systematic approach to change management
- Crisis situations require immediate stabilization and simplified decision-making protocols
- Maintaining couple connection during transitions requires modified expectations and intentional effort
- Growth opportunities within transitions can strengthen relationships and build resilience for future challenges

Chapter 16: Creating a sensory sanctuary together

Your home becomes the foundation where both partners can truly exist without masking or pretending. When one person needs complete silence to process their day and another craves the steady hum of background noise, the challenge isn't insurmountable—it requires intentional design and mutual understanding.

The sensory environment you create together will either support your relationship or create daily friction. This chapter provides the framework for building spaces that honor both partners' neurological needs while fostering connection and intimacy.

Home as haven: Designing for neurodivergent needs

Creating a sensory sanctuary starts with understanding that your home serves as more than shelter—it functions as a recovery space, a recharge station, and a place where both partners can unmask safely. Traditional home design rarely considers sensory processing differences, but your space must work differently.

Case Example: Sarah and Marcus Sarah, who has ADHD, needs visual stimulation and prefers bright colors, multiple textures, and organized chaos that sparks her creativity. Marcus, autistic, requires minimal visual input, neutral colors, and clean lines to prevent overwhelm. Their first shared apartment became a source of daily stress when Sarah's colorful art supplies scattered across surfaces while Marcus felt bombarded by visual noise.

The solution came through zone-based design. They designated the living room as a neutral space with calming colors and minimal decoration, while Sarah's home office burst with color and creative materials. Marcus claimed the bedroom as his sanctuary with blackout curtains, soft textures, and complete organization systems.

The kitchen presented their biggest challenge until they implemented the "one surface" rule—only one counter could hold items at any time, rotating based on current needs. This satisfied Sarah's need for accessible supplies while maintaining Marcus's requirement for visual calm.

Case Example: Jordan and Alex Jordan experiences sensory seeking behaviors and needs movement, music, and tactile input throughout the day. Alex has sensory sensitivities and requires quiet, dim lighting, and minimal touch. Their studio apartment initially felt like a battleground between competing needs.

They solved this through temporal zoning—the same space served different sensory functions at different times. Mornings belonged to Alex's quiet routine with soft lighting and minimal sound. Afternoons became Jordan's time for music, movement, and creative projects. Evenings returned to calm with negotiated background sounds that satisfied both partners.

The key breakthrough came when they installed adjustable lighting systems, sound-dampening panels that could be repositioned, and furniture that served multiple functions. A simple ottoman opened to store Jordan's fidget toys while providing Alex's preferred seating texture.

Zone creation: Spaces for different sensory states

Effective sensory zoning doesn't require a mansion—it requires strategic thinking about how spaces can serve multiple needs without compromise. Each zone should have a clear sensory purpose while maintaining flexibility for changing needs.

The Calm Zone This space prioritizes sensory regulation and recovery. Soft lighting, minimal visual input, comfortable seating, and sound control create an environment where overwhelmed nervous systems can reset. Both partners need access to this zone, though they might use it differently.

Essential elements include adjustable lighting from bright task lighting to dim ambient options, sound control through white noise machines or noise-canceling capabilities, comfortable seating that supports different body needs, and temperature control since sensory sensitivity often includes thermal regulation challenges.

The Stimulation Zone Some neurodivergent individuals need sensory input to regulate, focus, or feel comfortable. This zone provides safe opportunities for sensory seeking without overwhelming sensitive partners.

Include textured surfaces, bright or colorful elements, music or sound systems, movement opportunities like fidget tools or exercise equipment, and creative supplies that can be contained but accessible.

The Transition Zone Often overlooked, transition zones help partners shift between different sensory states. The entryway, for example, should provide a buffer between the outside world and your sanctuary.

Case Example: River and Cam River needs deep pressure input and seeks out weighted blankets, tight hugs, and firm surfaces. Cam experiences touch sensitivity and needs control over physical contact. Their bedroom initially created nightly conflicts as River sought physical connection while Cam needed space to decompress.

They redesigned their bedroom with separate but connected sleeping arrangements. River's side included a weighted blanket, firm mattress, and textured throws. Cam's side featured soft, breathable fabrics, adjustable firmness, and a small side table for sensory tools like noise-canceling earbuds or eye masks.

The breakthrough came with their "connection corner"—a designated space with a large, comfortable chair where they could choose different types of physical closeness. Sometimes Cam would lean against River for deep pressure they both enjoyed. Other times, they sat side by side with minimal contact but maintained emotional connection through conversation or shared activities.

The compromise equation: Meeting conflicting sensory needs

True compromise in sensory design doesn't mean both partners sacrifice their needs—it means finding creative solutions that honor both neurotypes simultaneously. This requires moving beyond either/or thinking toward both/and solutions.

Light Solutions When one partner needs bright light for focus and energy while the other requires dim lighting to prevent overwhelm, standard lighting fails both. Layer your lighting with multiple sources, adjustable brightness levels, and directional options.

Install dimmer switches on all overhead lights, add task lighting for focused work, use colored bulbs that can adjust from cool to warm tones, and create lighting zones that can operate independently.

Sound Management Sound conflicts often create the most immediate stress. One partner might need complete silence while the other requires background noise for concentration or comfort.

Use white noise machines that can be directed away from sensitive partners, install sound-absorbing materials like rugs, curtains, or acoustic panels, create physical barriers that reduce sound transmission, and establish quiet hours that both partners can rely on.

Noise-canceling headphones become relationship tools, not isolation devices. When one partner needs silence and the other needs sound, headphones allow both needs to coexist in shared spaces.

Temperature Control Sensory processing differences often include thermal sensitivity. One partner might always feel cold while the other overheats easily. Layer your temperature solutions with multiple heating and cooling options, breathable and insulating fabric choices, and personal climate control tools.

Sensory joy sharing: Finding mutual sensory pleasures

While accommodating differences matters, discovering shared sensory experiences that both partners enjoy creates connection and intimacy. These mutual pleasures become relationship strengths rather than areas requiring compromise.

Case Example: Quinn and Reese Quinn experiences auditory processing differences and struggles with certain frequencies but finds deep bass sounds soothing. Reese has ADHD and uses music for emotional regulation but prefers high-energy beats. They discovered their shared love for ambient electronic music with strong bass lines and minimal vocals.

This discovery led to evening rituals where they listened to carefully curated playlists while doing separate activities in the same room. Quinn would organize collections or work on detailed projects while Reese sketched or planned creative projects. The shared sound environment supported both their individual needs while creating emotional connection.

They expanded this principle to other sensory experiences, finding scented candles with earthy bases that didn't trigger Quinn's scent sensitivities while providing Reese with the sensory input they craved.

Movement and Touch Partners can find shared sensory experiences through movement activities that accommodate different needs. Dancing might work for some couples, while others prefer walking, swimming, or simple stretching routines done together.

Touch preferences require careful navigation, but many couples discover forms of physical connection that satisfy both partners. Some enjoy parallel touch—sitting close without demanding physical interaction. Others find specific types of touch that provide comfort for both partners.

Guest protocols: Maintaining sanctuary with visitors

Your sensory sanctuary needs protection from well-meaning visitors who might not understand neurodivergent needs. This requires clear protocols that maintain your space's function while accommodating social connections.

Preparation Strategies Before guests arrive, discuss sensory challenges they might unknowingly create. Loud conversations, strong scents, unexpected sounds, or changes to your established systems can disrupt carefully maintained balance.

Create guest guidelines that protect your sensory environment without seeming unwelcoming. This might include requesting minimal perfume or cologne, establishing quiet hours, explaining your lighting preferences, or providing headphones for guests who want to listen to music.

Recovery Plans Even with preparation, social visits can overwhelm sensory systems. Plan recovery time and space for after guests leave. This might mean immediate access to your calm zone, pre-planned sensory regulation activities, or simply understanding that both partners might need extra processing time.

Case Example: Avery and Taylor Avery has autism and requires several hours to recover after social interactions, needing complete quiet and minimal stimulation. Taylor has ADHD and feels energized by social connections but crashes hard afterward, needing movement and creative outlets.

They developed a post-social protocol that honored both recovery styles. Immediately after guests left, Avery retreated to their bedroom with noise-canceling headphones and a favorite book. Taylor went to their home gym space or worked on art projects. After individual recovery time, they reconnected over a simple shared meal and discussed positive moments from their social time.

This protocol eliminated the post-social arguments that used to occur when their different recovery needs created conflict.

Evolution and adjustment: Adapting spaces over time

Sensory needs change with stress levels, life circumstances, hormonal fluctuations, and personal growth. Your sanctuary must adapt accordingly without requiring complete redesigns every time needs shift.

Flexible Systems Build adaptability into your design choices. Modular furniture can be rearranged for different needs. Adjustable lighting, removable sound dampening, and storage systems that can be reorganized allow your space to grow with changing requirements.

Regular Assessment Schedule quarterly reviews of your sensory environment. Discuss what's working, what needs adjustment, and any new challenges that have emerged. These conversations prevent small irritations from building into relationship conflicts.

Seasonal Adjustments Many neurodivergent individuals experience seasonal changes in sensory processing. Winter might require different lighting solutions, while summer heat could necessitate cooling strategies. Plan for these predictable changes rather than waiting for problems to emerge.

Case Example: Morgan and Casey Morgan's sensory sensitivities increase significantly during stressful work periods, requiring more quiet space and minimal visual input. Casey's ADHD symptoms intensify during busy seasons, creating greater need for stimulation and movement.

They created a "stress protocol" that temporarily modified their shared spaces during high-pressure periods. During Morgan's work crises, they moved colorful artwork to Casey's office and added extra sound-dampening to shared areas. During Casey's intense creative periods, they set up a temporary movement area in the living room and established longer quiet times for Morgan.

These temporary adjustments prevented their stress periods from destroying their carefully designed sanctuary. They knew the changes were temporary and had clear plans for returning to their baseline setup.

Quick sensory fixes under $20

Simple, inexpensive modifications can dramatically improve your sensory environment without major renovations or significant financial investment.

Lighting Solutions Replace standard bulbs with adjustable LED options that range from cool to warm light. Add lamp shades or filters to existing fixtures to soften harsh light. Use string lights to create gentle ambient lighting options.

Sound Management Download white noise apps or purchase small sound machines. Hang heavy curtains or tapestries to absorb sound. Use draft stoppers under doors to reduce sound transmission between rooms.

Texture and Comfort Add textured throw pillows or blankets to provide tactile input options. Use removable adhesive strips to create textured surfaces on walls or furniture. Purchase weighted lap pads for pressure input that doesn't require full weighted blankets.

Organization and Visual Calm Use baskets or boxes to contain visual clutter while keeping items accessible. Add plants that provide visual interest without overwhelming sensitive systems. Create designated spots for frequently used items to reduce search stress.

Action steps for implementation

Start with one zone rather than attempting to redesign your entire home simultaneously. Choose the space where you spend the most time together and focus your initial efforts there.

1. **Conduct a sensory audit** of your current space, noting what supports and what challenges each partner

2. **Identify your highest priority needs** that currently create the most daily friction
3. **Choose three small modifications** you can implement immediately with minimal cost or effort
4. **Plan one major zone adjustment** that addresses your most significant sensory conflict
5. **Establish a review schedule** for assessing and adjusting your sensory environment

Moving forward together

Your home should support your relationship rather than creating daily obstacles. When both partners can exist comfortably in shared spaces, energy previously spent managing sensory challenges becomes available for connection, intimacy, and growth.

The sanctuary you create together reflects your commitment to understanding and accommodating each other's neurological differences. This investment in your shared environment pays dividends in reduced daily stress and increased relationship satisfaction.

Key Takeaways

- Design your home as a recovery space where both partners can unmask safely and comfortably
- Create distinct zones that serve different sensory functions while maintaining flexibility for changing needs
- Find creative both/and solutions rather than compromising away either partner's essential requirements
- Discover shared sensory experiences that create connection while honoring individual differences
- Protect your sanctuary through clear guest protocols and recovery planning
- Build adaptability into your design to accommodate changing needs and circumstances
- Start small with inexpensive modifications before making major changes

- Regular assessment and adjustment prevent small issues from becoming relationship conflicts

Chapter 17: Long-term love with AuDHD

Neurodivergent relationships don't follow the traditional relationship timeline that mainstream culture expects. Your connection might intensify quickly through shared special interests, then require months of parallel processing before deepening again. This isn't relationship failure—it's neurodivergent love finding its own rhythm.

Long-term success requires understanding how AuDHD traits affect relationship evolution over time. The same characteristics that created your initial connection will continue shaping your partnership, but their expression changes as you grow together and individually.

The long game: How AuDHD relationships evolve

Neurotypical relationship advice often focuses on maintaining excitement and preventing complacency, but neurodivergent partnerships operate differently. Your relationship might appear stable from the outside while experiencing rich internal growth that others can't observe.

Intensity Cycles Many AuDHD couples experience natural cycles of intense connection followed by periods of parallel existence. Rather than indicating relationship problems, these cycles often reflect healthy accommodation of different processing styles and energy levels.

During intense connection phases, partners might share special interests obsessively, communicate constantly, or spend all available time together. This intensity isn't sustainable long-term, nor should it be. The parallel phases that follow allow individual processing, special interest exploration, and nervous system regulation.

Case Example: Sam and Riley Sam has autism and experiences relationship connection through shared learning and deep conversations about specific topics. Riley has ADHD and connects through shared activities and physical presence. Their relationship intensity peaked during Riley's hyperfocus periods on topics that matched Sam's special interests.

During their first year together, Riley became obsessed with marine biology, which had been Sam's passion since childhood. They spent months visiting aquariums, reading research papers together, and discussing ocean ecosystems for hours each evening. Their connection felt profound and unbreakable.

When Riley's interest shifted to sustainable architecture, Sam initially feared relationship abandonment. They interpreted Riley's decreased marine biology enthusiasm as rejection of their shared connection. However, they learned to appreciate how Riley's shifting focuses brought new knowledge and experiences to their relationship while Sam's steady interests provided continuity and depth.

Over five years together, they established a rhythm where Riley's intense focuses lasted 3-6 months while Sam maintained 2-3 core interests consistently. This pattern created natural cycles of intense shared exploration followed by parallel pursuit periods. Rather than threatening their connection, these cycles enriched their relationship by preventing stagnation while honoring both their neurological patterns.

Growth Through Special Interests Long-term AuDHD relationships often develop around evolving special interests rather than traditional milestones like anniversaries or achievements. Partners might measure relationship growth through shared learning experiences, mastered skills, or deepened understanding of complex topics.

This growth pattern confuses outside observers who expect relationships to develop through social milestones, but it reflects genuine neurodivergent connection. Partners who support each other's intense interests create bonds based on acceptance and enthusiasm rather than social expectations.

Passion patterns: Maintaining spark with attention differences

Maintaining romantic and sexual connection requires understanding how ADHD and autism affect desire, arousal, and intimate communication. Traditional relationship advice about spontaneity and variety might conflict with autistic needs for predictability and routine.

Case Example: Alex and Jordan Alex has autism and experiences sexual desire predictably, preferring familiar routines and consistent timing. Jordan has ADHD and experiences fluctuating libido tied to attention cycles, stress levels, and hyperfocus periods. Their intimate life initially suffered from mismatched expectations and communication difficulties.

Alex interpreted Jordan's inconsistent interest as personal rejection, while Jordan felt pressured by Alex's routine expectations. They solved this through intentional communication and accommodation strategies.

They established "intimacy check-ins" every few days where they discussed current interest levels, energy states, and preferences without pressure for immediate action. This removed the guesswork and rejection sensitivity that had been damaging their connection.

Alex learned to recognize Jordan's hyperfocus periods as times when sexual interest naturally decreased, while Jordan appreciated Alex's need for predictable intimate connection. They developed flexible routines that provided Alex with consistency while accommodating Jordan's fluctuating availability.

Their breakthrough came when they separated physical affection from sexual expectation. Regular physical touch, cuddling, and sensory connection continued regardless of sexual interest levels. This reduced performance pressure while maintaining intimate bonds.

Sensory Considerations in Intimacy Long-term AuDHD couples must navigate changing sensory needs that affect physical intimacy. Sensitivities might increase during stress periods, while sensory-seeking behaviors might intensify during certain relationship phases.

Communication about sensory preferences becomes ongoing rather than one-time conversations. Partners need permission to communicate changing needs without fear of disappointing each other.

Case Example: Casey and Morgan Casey experiences touch sensitivity that fluctuates with stress levels and hormonal changes. During low-stress periods, they enjoyed varied physical touch and spontaneous intimacy. During high-stress times, touch could feel overwhelming or even painful.

Morgan has ADHD and craves physical stimulation for emotional regulation and connection. They initially took Casey's touch aversion personally, interpreting it as relationship rejection rather than sensory overwhelm.

They developed a communication system using simple signals to indicate current touch preferences without lengthy explanations. Green meant full touch availability, yellow indicated gentle touch only, and red meant minimal physical contact needed.

This system eliminated the emotional processing required to explain sensory states repeatedly while giving Morgan clear information about Casey's current needs. Morgan learned alternative ways to connect emotionally during red periods, while Casey felt safe communicating boundaries without fear of disappointing their partner.

Over time, they discovered that acknowledging and accommodating Casey's sensory fluctuations actually increased overall physical intimacy. Casey felt safer being physically available during green periods when they knew their boundaries would be respected during challenging times.

Growing together: Supporting individual evolution

Neurodivergent individuals often experience significant personal growth and change throughout their lives as they better understand their neurotype and develop effective strategies. Long-term relationships must accommodate this evolution while maintaining connection.

Supporting Special Interest Evolution Partners' special interests will change over time, and these changes affect relationship dynamics. One partner might develop new passions that don't include their significant other, or might lose interest in previously shared activities.

Healthy AuDHD relationships view special interest evolution as individual growth rather than relationship threat. Partners support each other's changing interests while maintaining their own autonomy and development.

Case Example: River and Sage River's special interest in vintage motorcycles had been central to their identity and relationship for three years. Sage learned about engines, attended bike shows, and shared River's enthusiasm for restoration projects. Their garage became a shared workspace where they spent most weekends.

When River's interest shifted to sustainable urban planning, Sage initially felt abandoned. The garage sat unused while River spent hours reading policy papers and attending city council meetings. Sage worried they had lost their primary connection point and didn't understand River's new passion.

Rather than demanding River maintain their motorcycle interest, Sage supported this evolution while developing their own interests more fully. They took over the garage space for woodworking projects and found their own enthusiasm for handcrafted furniture.

This transition period challenged their relationship as they established new ways of connecting. They learned to share their separate interests through storytelling and education rather than joint participation. River would explain urban planning concepts to Sage, who shared woodworking techniques and project progress.

After two years, their relationship had deepened through this individual growth. They maintained strong emotional connection while pursuing separate passions, and occasionally found intersection points where Sage's furniture skills supported River's community development projects.

Masking and Unmasking Cycles Long-term relationships witness partners' masking patterns as they become more comfortable with authenticity. This process isn't linear—partners might unmask more during certain periods, then increase masking during stressful times or social demands.

Supporting each other through unmasking requires understanding that increased authenticity might temporarily disrupt relationship patterns. Partners might communicate differently, have different social needs, or express emotions more directly.

The familiarity factor: Comfort vs. taking for granted

Neurodivergent individuals often thrive on predictability and routine, but long-term relationships risk becoming so predictable that partners stop actively appreciating each other. Finding balance between comfortable routine and continued growth requires intentional effort.

Routine as Relationship Strength Many AuDHD couples discover that routines support their relationship rather than limiting it. Predictable patterns reduce decision fatigue, accommodate sensory needs, and create reliable connection points.

However, routines require conscious cultivation rather than unconscious habit. Partners must regularly assess whether their patterns still serve their relationship or have become empty habits.

Case Example: Avery and Blake Avery and Blake established strong daily routines early in their relationship that supported both their autism and ADHD needs. They had consistent wake-up times, meal patterns, and evening activities that created stability and reduced daily decision-making stress.

After three years, they realized their routines had become so automatic that they barely interacted meaningfully during their structured time together. They ate dinner while scrolling phones, watched familiar shows without discussion, and followed bedtime routines without connection.

They modified their routines to include intentional connection points. Dinner became phone-free time for sharing daily experiences. They established "curiosity time" where they asked each other questions about current interests or thoughts. Their bedtime routine included brief physical affection and verbal appreciation.

These modifications maintained the routine structure they needed while ensuring continued emotional connection. They preserved the predictability that supported their neurotypes while preventing relationship stagnation.

Appreciation Practice Long-term AuDHD relationships benefit from structured appreciation practices that counteract the tendency to focus on problems or take positive aspects for granted.

Regular appreciation doesn't require elaborate gestures or emotional expression that might feel uncomfortable for some neurodivergent individuals. Simple acknowledgment of specific behaviors, traits, or contributions maintains positive focus.

Milestone reimagined: Celebrating in AuDHD style

Traditional relationship milestones might not resonate with neurodivergent couples who measure relationship success differently. Creating your own celebration patterns that reflect your actual values and interests strengthens long-term connection.

Special Interest Anniversaries Rather than only celebrating relationship start dates, AuDHD couples might mark anniversaries of shared discoveries, learned skills, or completed projects. These celebrations honor the actual experiences that bond them together.

Case Example: Quinn and Taylor Quinn and Taylor realized that traditional anniversary celebrations felt forced and uncomfortable for both of them. They preferred small gatherings to large parties, valued shared learning over romantic gestures, and measured relationship success through personal growth rather than social recognition.

They created celebration patterns that reflected their authentic preferences. They marked the anniversary of their first shared special interest discovery, celebrated completing major projects together, and acknowledged personal growth milestones each partner achieved with the other's support.

These celebrations might involve visiting museums related to current interests, taking classes together, or simply spending extended time exploring topics they both enjoyed. The celebrations felt meaningful because they reflected their actual relationship experience rather than external expectations.

Achievement Recognition Many neurodivergent individuals don't naturally celebrate their accomplishments or might minimize achievements that required significant effort. Long-term partners can provide essential acknowledgment and appreciation for individual growth and success.

This recognition becomes particularly important for accomplishments that others might not understand or appreciate. Partners can celebrate communication breakthroughs, sensory regulation successes, or social interaction achievements that represent real growth.

Legacy building: Creating your unique love story

Long-term AuDHD relationships create their own legacy through the unique accommodations, understanding, and growth they generate together. This legacy might not resemble traditional relationship goals, but it reflects genuine partnership and mutual support.

Knowledge Legacy Many neurodivergent couples create extensive shared knowledge through their combined special interests and learning experiences. This intellectual legacy might include collections, research, creative works, or expertise that reflects their partnership.

Case Example: Dakota and Cameron Dakota's special interest in historical textiles combined with Cameron's ADHD-driven enthusiasm for hands-on learning created a unique partnership legacy. Over eight years together, they researched historical techniques, learned traditional crafts, and created museum-quality reproductions of historical garments.

Their legacy included not just the physical items they created, but the knowledge they accumulated and shared with others. They taught workshops, wrote articles, and mentored other couples who shared similar interests. Their relationship became a model for how neurodivergent partnerships could create meaningful contributions to their communities.

This legacy felt authentic to both partners because it grew from their genuine interests rather than external expectations about what couples should accomplish together.

Advocacy and Visibility Some long-term AuDHD couples choose to share their relationship experiences to help other neurodivergent individuals find acceptance and understanding. This advocacy work becomes part of their relationship legacy and shared purpose.

Adaptation Legacy The accommodation strategies and communication systems that couples develop over time become valuable resources for other neurodivergent partnerships. These practical solutions represent real relationship wisdom earned through experience.

Keeping magic alive: Quick tips

Long-term relationships require ongoing attention to maintain emotional connection and appreciation. Simple practices can prevent stagnation while accommodating neurodivergent communication and expression styles.

Daily Appreciation Share one specific thing you appreciated about your partner each day. This might be a behavior, effort, or quality you noticed. Keep these appreciations concrete and behavior-focused rather than abstract.

Interest Sharing Spend 10-15 minutes weekly sharing current interests, discoveries, or learning with each other. This maintains connection with your partner's internal world even when your interests don't overlap.

Sensory Check-ins Regularly ask about sensory needs, stress levels, and energy states. This information helps you support each other better and prevents sensory issues from creating relationship conflicts.

Routine Refreshing Monthly assess your routines to ensure they still serve your relationship positively. Small modifications can maintain predictability while preventing stagnation.

Looking ahead with wisdom

Long-term AuDHD relationships require different maintenance than neurotypical partnerships, but they offer unique rewards through deep understanding, acceptance, and growth. The challenges you navigate together create genuine intimacy based on authentic accommodation rather than superficial compatibility.

Your relationship success isn't measured by external standards but by your mutual growth, happiness, and ability to support each other's authentic selves. The patterns you establish early in your relationship will continue evolving, but the foundation of acceptance and understanding provides stability for whatever changes emerge.

Key Takeaways

- AuDHD relationships naturally cycle through intense connection and parallel processing periods
- Sexual and romantic intimacy requires ongoing communication about changing sensory needs and interest levels
- Individual growth and special interest evolution strengthen rather than threaten healthy partnerships
- Comfortable routines support neurodivergent relationships when they include intentional connection points
- Create celebration patterns that reflect your authentic interests rather than external expectations
- Build relationship legacy through shared knowledge, advocacy, or accommodation wisdom
- Simple daily practices maintain emotional connection while accommodating communication differences
- Success is measured by mutual growth and authentic support rather than social milestones

Chapter 18: Your authentic love story

Every neurodivergent relationship represents a unique experiment in love, acceptance, and growth. The strategies, accommodations, and understanding you've developed together create a template that reflects your specific neurotypes, interests, and values rather than generic relationship advice.

This final chapter helps you integrate everything you've learned into a coherent approach that will continue guiding your relationship through future challenges and growth. Your authentic love story isn't about perfection—it's about conscious partnership that honors both individuals while building something meaningful together.

Integration station: Pulling it all together

Successful long-term relationships require systems that work consistently rather than strategies you remember only during crisis periods. The accommodations and communication patterns that support your partnership must become natural parts of your daily interaction.

Creating Your Relationship Operating System Think of your relationship as having an operating system—underlying processes that handle routine functions automatically while allowing conscious attention for new challenges or growth opportunities.

Your operating system includes your established communication patterns, sensory accommodations, conflict resolution approaches, and support strategies. These background processes should run smoothly most of the time, requiring conscious attention only when updates or troubleshooting become necessary.

Case Example: Phoenix and Sage Phoenix has autism and processes emotions slowly, needing time to understand their feelings before discussing relationship issues. Sage has ADHD and experiences emotions intensely in the moment, wanting immediate processing and resolution.

Over four years, they developed an operating system that accommodated both processing styles. When relationship issues arose, Sage could express immediate emotional reactions without expecting instant responses from Phoenix. Phoenix committed to revisiting conversations within 24-48 hours after processing time.

Their system included specific language patterns that worked for both partners. Sage learned to say "I'm having big feelings about this and need to share them, but I don't need you to respond right now" when beginning emotional discussions. Phoenix developed responses like "I hear you and need processing time before I can engage fully with this topic."

This operating system eliminated the relationship conflicts that previously occurred when their different processing styles created misunderstandings. Both partners felt heard and supported while honoring their neurological needs.

Regular System Updates Like computer operating systems, relationship systems require periodic updates to address new challenges, changing circumstances, or personal growth. Schedule regular relationship reviews to assess what's working and what needs adjustment.

These reviews shouldn't focus only on problems or conflicts. Spend equal time acknowledging successful strategies, appreciating positive changes, and planning for anticipated challenges.

Case Example: River and Alex River and Alex established quarterly relationship reviews that lasted 2-3 hours and followed a structured agenda. They discussed recent challenges and successes, assessed their communication patterns, reviewed their sensory accommodations, and planned for upcoming stressors or changes.

These reviews prevented small issues from becoming major conflicts while ensuring both partners felt heard and understood. They approached the reviews as collaborative problem-solving sessions rather than complaint sessions.

During one review, they realized that Alex's work stress was affecting their ability to communicate clearly about sensory needs. They developed specific strategies for high-stress periods, including simplified communication methods and temporary accommodation adjustments. Having these plans ready reduced relationship stress during Alex's challenging work periods.

Your relationship manifesto: Defining success your way

Mainstream culture promotes specific relationship goals and milestones that might not align with neurodivergent values or interests. Creating your own relationship manifesto helps you define success based on your actual priorities rather than external expectations.

Core Values Identification Your relationship manifesto should reflect the values that actually guide your partnership rather than values you think you should have. Neurodivergent couples often prioritize acceptance, growth, learning, and authenticity over traditional romantic ideals.

Consider what your relationship provides for each partner. This might include emotional safety, intellectual stimulation, sensory accommodation, personal growth support, or shared interest exploration. These benefits become the foundation for measuring relationship success.

Case Example: Casey and Morgan Casey and Morgan realized that traditional relationship advice about maintaining romance and excitement didn't resonate with their actual experience or desires. They valued intellectual connection, personal growth support, and comfortable predictability over spontaneity and romantic gestures.

Their relationship manifesto included commitments to supporting each other's special interests, maintaining individual autonomy, creating sensory-friendly shared spaces, and providing emotional safety for unmasking. They measured success through personal growth, learning achievements, and mutual support rather than social milestones.

This manifesto guided their decisions about social obligations, family expectations, and future planning. When relatives questioned their unconventual celebration patterns or lifestyle choices, they could refer to their clearly defined values and priorities.

Success Metrics That Matter Define specific ways to measure whether your relationship is meeting your stated values and goals. These metrics should be observable and meaningful to both partners rather than abstract ideals.

Examples might include frequency of meaningful conversations, successful navigation of sensory challenges, individual growth achievements, shared learning experiences, or effective conflict resolution instances.

Manifesto Evolution Your relationship manifesto will change as you grow individually and together. Regular reviews ensure that your stated values continue reflecting your actual priorities and experiences.

Case Example: Avery and Jordan Avery and Jordan's initial relationship manifesto focused heavily on accommodation and understanding as they learned to navigate their different neurotypes. After three years together, their updated manifesto included goals for community involvement, creative collaboration, and mutual advocacy.

This evolution reflected their growth from focusing on internal relationship dynamics to considering how their partnership could contribute to broader neurodivergent community support. Their values had expanded beyond personal accommodation to include social impact and visibility.

The growth mindset: Continuous learning in love

Neurodivergent relationships benefit from approaching partnership as an ongoing learning experience rather than a problem to solve once and forget. Both partners continue developing throughout their lives, and your relationship must accommodate this continued evolution.

Individual Growth Support Long-term relationships require balancing couple identity with individual development. Partners need permission and support to pursue personal interests, develop new skills, and change in ways that affect the relationship dynamic.

Supporting individual growth sometimes means accepting changes that create temporary relationship challenges. A partner who learns to mask less might communicate differently or have different social needs. Someone who develops new special interests might shift time and attention allocation.

Learning From Challenges Every relationship difficulty provides information about your partnership dynamics, individual needs, or accommodation strategies. Approaching problems as learning opportunities rather than failures creates a growth-oriented relationship culture.

This doesn't mean minimizing legitimate concerns or accepting harmful behaviors. It means viewing challenges as data that can improve your relationship understanding and effectiveness.

Case Example: Quinn and Blake Quinn discovered they had been masking significantly more than they realized, even within their relationship with Blake. As Quinn began unmasking more authentically, their communication style changed, their sensory needs increased, and their social preferences shifted.

These changes initially created relationship stress as Blake adjusted to Quinn's more direct communication and decreased social availability. Rather than viewing these changes as relationship problems, they approached them as learning opportunities about Quinn's authentic needs and preferences.

Blake learned to appreciate Quinn's direct communication style and found ways to meet their own social needs that didn't require Quinn's participation. Quinn developed better ways to communicate their changing needs and energy levels. Their relationship ultimately became more authentic and satisfying for both partners.

Knowledge Integration The information you learn about neurodivergence, relationships, and individual development should be integrated into your partnership approach rather than remaining abstract concepts.

Read research together, attend workshops or support groups, and discuss how new information applies to your specific relationship dynamics. This shared learning creates common understanding and vocabulary for discussing your experiences.

Community and support: Building your village

Neurodivergent relationships often exist in isolation from mainstream relationship models and support systems. Building community with other neurodivergent individuals and supportive allies provides validation, resources, and practical advice.

Finding Your People Look for community among other neurodivergent individuals who understand your experiences without extensive explanation. This might include online communities, local support groups, professional organizations, or interest-based groups where you're likely to find other neurodivergent individuals.

Case Example: Dakota and Sam Dakota and Sam felt isolated in their relationship experiences until they found a local neurodivergent couples support group. Meeting other partnerships that navigated similar challenges provided validation and practical strategies they hadn't considered.

The group shared accommodation strategies, communication techniques, and advocacy approaches that members had developed through their own experiences. This shared knowledge accelerated

Dakota and Sam's relationship development and reduced their sense of being unusual or problematic.

They also discovered that their relationship strengths—deep acceptance, creative problem-solving, and intellectual connection—were common among neurodivergent couples. This recognition helped them appreciate their partnership rather than focusing only on challenges.

Support Network Development Build relationships with individuals who understand and support your neurodivergent needs. This might include healthcare providers, therapists, friends, family members, or community members who provide practical and emotional support.

Your support network should include people who understand both partners' needs and can provide assistance during challenging periods. This network becomes particularly important during health crises, work stress, or major life transitions.

Reciprocal Support As you develop effective relationship strategies and accommodations, consider sharing your knowledge with other neurodivergent individuals who might benefit from your experiences. This creates reciprocal support networks where everyone contributes and receives assistance.

Advocacy in action: Being visible for others

Many neurodivergent couples choose to share their relationship experiences to help other individuals find acceptance, understanding, and practical strategies. This advocacy work can become part of your shared purpose and legacy.

Representation Matters Positive examples of successful neurodivergent relationships provide hope and practical models for individuals who struggle to find acceptance or understanding. Your visibility can help others recognize that authentic partnership is possible.

This representation doesn't require public speaking or formal advocacy work. Simple visibility in your community, honest discussions with friends and family, or sharing experiences in appropriate settings can provide valuable representation.

Case Example: River and Casey River and Casey began sharing their relationship story after realizing how few positive neurodivergent relationship examples they had encountered when they were struggling with early relationship challenges.

They started by speaking honestly with friends and family about their accommodation strategies and relationship strengths. This led to speaking at local support groups and eventually presenting workshops for other couples.

Their advocacy work strengthened their own relationship by requiring them to articulate their strategies clearly and celebrate their successes publicly. It also provided meaning and purpose that extended beyond their individual partnership.

Educational Opportunities Share information about neurodivergence and relationship accommodation with receptive audiences. This might include correcting misconceptions, providing practical examples, or educating professionals who work with neurodivergent individuals.

Educational advocacy helps create more supportive environments for all neurodivergent individuals while building your expertise and confidence in discussing your experiences.

Writing your future: Next chapters of your story

Your relationship will continue evolving as you both grow individually and together. Planning for future challenges and opportunities while remaining flexible enough to accommodate unexpected changes requires ongoing attention and communication.

Anticipating Life Transitions Major life changes—career shifts, health challenges, family changes, housing moves, or aging—will test your relationship systems and require adaptation of your established patterns.

Discuss how you want to handle anticipated transitions while recognizing that your actual response might differ from your plans. Having general approaches and values clarified provides guidance during stressful transition periods.

Case Example: Phoenix and Sage Phoenix and Sage knew that starting a family would significantly challenge their carefully established relationship patterns and sensory accommodations. Rather than avoiding planning because they couldn't predict specific challenges, they discussed their general approaches and values.

They clarified their commitment to maintaining individual sensory needs even during child-rearing stress. They planned to modify rather than abandon their communication systems. They identified family and friends who could provide understanding support during difficult periods.

When their child was born with their own neurodivergent traits, Phoenix and Sage's advance planning helped them adapt their family systems to accommodate three different neurotypes rather than abandoning their relationship needs entirely.

Dreams and Goals Share your individual and relationship dreams regularly. These might include travel goals, learning objectives, creative projects, career aspirations, or community involvement plans.

Supporting each other's dreams while building shared goals creates forward momentum and prevents relationship stagnation. Some dreams will change or become impossible, but discussing them maintains connection with each other's internal worlds.

Legacy Planning Consider what you want your relationship to contribute to your families, communities, or broader society. This legacy might include the knowledge you develop, the advocacy work you do, the creative projects you complete, or simply the model you provide for authentic partnership.

Daily practices for thriving

Long-term relationship success requires consistent daily practices rather than dramatic gestures or major interventions. Simple routines that maintain connection, appreciation, and support create sustainable relationship satisfaction.

Morning Connection Start each day with brief connection that acknowledges your partnership. This might include physical affection, verbal appreciation, sharing daily plans, or simply making eye contact and checking in.

Keep morning routines simple and predictable rather than elaborate or varying. Consistency matters more than creativity for building sustainable connection patterns.

Evening Processing End days with some form of shared processing about your experiences. This might include discussing daily highlights, sharing challenges, expressing appreciation, or planning for tomorrow.

Evening processing helps partners stay connected with each other's internal experiences and provides opportunities to address small issues before they become larger problems.

Weekly Planning Spend time weekly discussing upcoming schedules, anticipated challenges, individual needs, and shared plans. This planning reduces daily decision-making stress while ensuring both partners' needs receive attention.

Weekly planning sessions also provide opportunities to assess relationship dynamics, celebrate successes, and make necessary adjustments to your systems.

Monthly Appreciation Dedicate time monthly to specifically appreciating your partner and relationship. This might include verbal appreciation, written notes, shared activities you both enjoy, or simple acknowledgment of your partnership growth.

Regular appreciation prevents taking positive aspects of your relationship for granted while building emotional reserves for challenging periods.

Closing reflections

Your neurodivergent love story represents courage, creativity, and commitment to authentic partnership. The accommodations you've developed, the understanding you've built, and the growth you've supported in each other create a unique template for love that honors both individuals while building something meaningful together.

The challenges you've navigated haven't made you stronger—they've made you more skilled at partnership. The differences you've learned to accommodate haven't brought you closer—they've taught you deeper acceptance. The growth you've supported in each other hasn't fixed anything—it's revealed the beauty of authentic development.

Your relationship succeeds not because you've overcome neurodivergence, but because you've learned to honor it. The strategies that work for you might not work for other couples, just as mainstream relationship advice hasn't worked for you. This specificity isn't a limitation—it's the foundation of genuine intimacy.

Continue writing your love story with consciousness, creativity, and commitment to each other's authentic selves. The chapters ahead will bring new challenges and opportunities, but you've developed the foundation for navigating whatever emerges together.

Your authentic love story matters not only for your own happiness, but as proof that neurodivergent individuals deserve and can create meaningful, lasting partnerships. Live your love story proudly, knowing that your visibility and success help others believe in their own possibilities for authentic connection.

Key Takeaways

- Integrate successful strategies into automatic relationship operating systems that require minimal conscious attention
- Define relationship success based on your authentic values rather than external expectations or mainstream milestones
- Approach partnership as continuous learning that accommodates individual growth and changing needs
- Build community with other neurodivergent individuals who understand your experiences and can provide practical support
- Consider sharing your relationship wisdom to help other neurodivergent individuals find acceptance and practical strategies
- Plan for future challenges while remaining flexible enough to accommodate unexpected changes and growth
- Establish simple daily, weekly, and monthly practices that maintain connection and appreciation consistently
- Celebrate your unique love story as proof that neurodivergent individuals can create meaningful, lasting partnerships

Reference

1. **Rong, Y., Yang, C. J., Jin, Y., & Wang, Y. (2021).** Prevalence of attention-deficit/hyperactivity disorder in individuals with autism spectrum disorder: A meta-analysis. *Research in Autism Spectrum Disorders*, 83, 101759.
2. **Antshel, K. M., Zhang-James, Y., Wagner, K. E., Ledesma, A., & Faraone, S. V. (2016).** An update on the comorbidity of ADHD and ASD: A focus on clinical management. *Expert Review of Neurotherapeutics*, 16(3), 279-293.
3. **Dodson, W. W. (2005).** Pharmacotherapy of adult ADHD. *Journal of Clinical Psychology*, 61(5), 589-606.
4. **Mowbray, T. (2020).** Rejection sensitive dysphoria as a common component of ADHD. *The Primary Care Companion for CNS Disorders*, 22(3), 19nr02551.
5. **Robertson, A. E., & Simmons, D. R. (2015).** The sensory experiences of adults with autism spectrum disorder: A qualitative analysis. *Perception*, 44(5), 569-586.
6. **Crane, L., Goddard, L., & Pring, L. (2009).** Sensory processing in adults with autism spectrum disorders. *Autism*, 13(3), 215-228.
7. **Heasman, B., & Gillespie, A. (2018).** Perspective-taking is two-sided: Misunderstandings between people with Asperger's syndrome and their family members. *Autism*, 22(6), 740-750.
8. **Sedgewick, F., Hill, V., Yates, R., Pickering, L., & Pellicano, E. (2016).** Gender differences in the social motivation and friendship experiences of autistic and non-autistic adolescents. *Journal of Autism and Developmental Disorders*, 46(4), 1297-1306.
9. **Hoover, D. W., & Kaufman, J. (2018).** Adverse childhood experiences in children with autism spectrum disorder. *Current Opinion in Psychiatry*, 31(2), 128-132.

10. **Rumball, F., Happé, F., & Grey, N. (2020).** Experience of trauma and PTSD symptoms in adults with autism spectrum disorders. *Research in Autism Spectrum Disorders*, 70, 101469.

11. **Demetriou, E. A., Lampit, A., Quintana, D. S., Naismith, S. L., Song, Y. J. C., Pye, J. E., ... & Guastella, A. J. (2018).** Autism spectrum disorders: A meta-analysis of executive function. *Molecular Psychiatry*, 23(5), 1198-1204.

12. **Craig, F., Margari, F., Legrottaglie, A. R., Palumbi, R., De Giambattista, C., & Margari, L. (2016).** A review of executive function deficits in autism spectrum disorder and attention-deficit/hyperactivity disorder. *Neuropsychiatric Disease and Treatment*, 12, 1191-1202.

13. **Hull, L., Petrides, K. V., Allison, C., Smith, P., Baron-Cohen, S., Lai, M. C., & Mandy, W. (2017).** "Putting on my best normal": Social camouflaging in adults with autism spectrum conditions. *Journal of Autism and Developmental Disorders*, 47(8), 2519-2534.

14. **Pecora, L. A., Mesibov, G. B., & Stokes, M. A. (2016).** Sexuality in high-functioning autism: A systematic review and meta-analysis. *Journal of Autism and Developmental Disorders*, 46(11), 3519-3556.

15. **Spain, D., Sin, J., Linder, K. B., McMahon, J., & Happé, F. (2018).** Social anxiety in autism spectrum disorder: A systematic review. *Research in Autism Spectrum Disorders*, 52, 51-68.

www.ingramcontent.com/pod-product-compliance
Lightning Source LLC
Chambersburg PA
CBHW060509090426
42735CB00011B/2156